PRESIDENTS
AT HOME

PRESIDENTS AT HOME

by Elizabeth Van Steenwyk

Illustrated with photographs

Julian Messner

New York

JULIAN MESSNER and colophon are trademarks of Simon & Schuster, registered in the U.S. Patent and Trademark Office.

Manufactured in the United States of America

Design by Philip Jaget

Library of Congress Cataloging in Publication Data

Van Steenwyk, Elizabeth.
    Presidents at home.

    1. Presidents—United States—Homes—Juvenile literature.   2. Presidents—United States—Biography—Juvenile literature.   I. Title.
E176.1.V36   973   80-36864
ISBN 0-671-34008-5

To Helen Hinckley Jones and the Thursday Night Regulars, whose constructive critique was a continuing source of assistance and inspiration.

The author gratefully acknowledges the assistance of Eileen Davis, Julie Boehm, and Karyn Hanrahan.

Contents

Introduction   8

1   George Washington   10
2   John Adams   15
3   Thomas Jefferson   18
4   James Madison   22
5   James Monroe   24
6   John Quincy Adams   27
7   Andrew Jackson   29
8   Martin Van Buren   32
9   William Henry Harrison   34
10   John Tyler   36
11   James K. Polk   38
12   Zachary Taylor   40
13   Millard Fillmore   42
14   Franklin Pierce   44
15   James Buchanan   46
16   Abraham Lincoln   48
17   Andrew Johnson   51
18   Ulysses S. Grant   54
19   Rutherford B. Hayes   59
20   James A. Garfield   61

21   Chester A. Arthur   63
22   Grover Cleveland   65
23   Benjamin Harrison   67
24   Grover Cleveland   65
25   William McKinley   70
26   Theodore Roosevelt   72
27   William Howard Taft   78
28   Woodrow Wilson   81
29   Warren G. Harding   86
30   Calvin Coolidge   89
31   Herbert Hoover   93
32   Franklin D. Roosevelt   97
33   Harry S. Truman   100
34   Dwight D. Eisenhower   102
35   John F. Kennedy   106
36   Lyndon B. Johnson   109
37   Richard M. Nixon   112
38   Gerald R. Ford   115
39   Jimmy Carter   118
    How To Get There   120

Introduction

Do you have a dollar bill in your pocket or piggy bank? Take it out and see whose picture is on it. Are there any stamps in your desk? You may discover a Presidential face on them. Perhaps there are pictures on the walls of your classroom. It's safe to say there will be at least one President there. Glance through the history books, magazines and newspapers in your home or library. Pictures of Presidents again! And again!

Presidential names are as popular as their faces. Think about parks, streets, towns, buildings and schools with which you may be familiar. Maybe you attend Kennedy School. Maybe you play in Washington Park. Perhaps your house is on Garfield Avenue. Do you live in Lincoln, Illinois or Jackson, Mississippi?

We remember our Presidents through their names, faces and achievements in office. However, there's one more way to remember them that you may not have thought about. We also keep their memories bright by preserving the homes in which they once lived.

A President's home tells us what his life was like before or after he moved into the one home all Presidents have in common—the one at 1600 Pennsylvania Avenue in Washington, D.C. Historical facts become real for us to see and touch. We can see a President's favorite chair, touch his childhood toys or books, perhaps even smell the same kind of flowers in his garden that he once did.

When we visit a President's home, we also find out how he lived in his time, and whether he was rich or poor. Did he read by candlelight or electric light? Were the floors of his home covered with imported carpets or hand-hewn planks? Were the messages of the day carried by horseback or telephone? Did he bathe in an icy creek or a bathtub?

When we travel to a President's home, we see it in a special setting, too. It may be in the North or South. It may be in the city or country. The President may have played on city streets or in his father's cornfields. His family may have been Confederates during the Civil War.

The home of the President may have influenced what he would say in his campaigns. Presidents who were born in log cabins became "log cabin" candidates. If candidates did not travel during a campaign, voters came to them instead. These were known as "front porch" campaigns.

In the next chapters, we're going to visit thirty-five Presidential homes. (There are no homes for Presidents Ford and Carter right now. And there is no home for President McKinley.)

In the last chapter, travel information is given for all of the homes which we will visit. Several Presidents left more than one, and those are listed, too.

Now it's time to visit our Presidents at home.

1. George Washington

The welcome mat is always out at Mount Vernon. George Washington put it there in 1794 when he wrote, "I have no objection to any sober or orderly person's gratifying their curiosity in viewing the buildings, gardens and etc. about Mount Vernon."

The first President loved his land, and considered himself a farmer before he was a soldier, statesman, leader, politician or diplomat. "Agriculture," he wrote, "has ever been among the most favored of my amusements."

He was in his early twenties when he inherited the two-thousand-acre plantation from his older brother, Lawrence. His father, Augustine, had already built the central portion of the mansion on the land which had been in the Washington family since 1674.

Now young George set out to enlarge the house as well as increase the land holdings. In time, he would own eight thousand acres along the Potomac River in Virginia. But before he could do much, he was called to service in the French and Indian Wars and spent six years away from home.

However, his thoughts were never far away. He sent back instructions to his neighbor, Mr. Fairfax, to raise the one-story house to two-and-a-half stories. He instructed his overseer to re-decorate it throughout. This had been completed when he returned with his bride, Martha Custis, in 1759.

The Colonel (Washington's rank during the French and Indian Wars) continued to build his estate and mansion carefully. In those days, large estates seemed like small villages because so many people lived on them. About 90 people lived at Mt. Vernon, and they were needed for the many jobs that had to be done by hand.

Washington had the kitchen joined to the main house with a covered walkway. Then he added rooms at both ends of the house. Next he laid out formal gardens and service lanes.

The kitchen was often a separate building on plantations and farms of the eighteenth century. This kitchen occupies the site of the original one at Wakefield, Washington's birthplace, near Fredericksburg, Virginia. The apples, potatoes and even the grain for the bread were grown and processed right on the plantation. Cooking was done in the wood-burning fireplace in the back. (National Park Service)

Service lanes were walking or riding paths which led to small buildings around the main house. Work went on in each of the small buildings that was important to everyday life on the estate. One building contained the smokehouse where the cook preserved the meat by smoking it. (Refrigeration had not yet been invented.) In the spinning house, ten or more women spun or knit material for clothes. Other buildings were the washhouse where the laundress worked and a coachhouse where the coaches were kept spotlessly clean.

In 1773, as Washington began to enlarge his house once more, he was called away again. This time he went to Philadelphia to serve in the First and Second Continental Congresses. Finally, he was appointed Commander-in-Chief during the Revolutionary War. For eight more years, the General could only supervise the expansion of his home through letters. His cousin, Lund Washington, added the banquet hall and the piazza (an open porch or portico at the front of the house) following the General's written instructions. During the siege of Yorktown in September and October of 1781, General Washington was able to visit his home which was not far away.

In 1783, the war ended and he resigned his commission, returning to Mount Vernon on Christmas Eve. "At length I have become a private citizen on the banks of the Potomac," he wrote to a friend.

Soon he was ordering materials for a stable for his horses, flagstones for the eight-columned piazza and furnishings for the banquet room. In 1787, the cupola (a small dome) was finished and put in place on the roof, with a dove of peace for a weathervane. Mount Vernon was finished.

Mount Vernon, the Virginia plantation home of George Washington. It was built in 1743, and named in honor of Edward Vernon, a British admiral, under whom Lawrence Washington served. George Washington took possession of the estate in 1754, enlarged the house and developed the plantation into one of the finest in all the South. To support the mansion's many activities, Washington built a village-like group of nearby service buildings, most of which still exist. (Virginia State Travel Service)

The new country called Washington to serve again in 1789 as its first President. During his two terms of office, he was able to return to Mount Vernon only twice a year. In 1797, after refusing a third term as President, George Washington came home again. "I can truly say I had rather be at Mount Vernon . . ." he wrote to a friend.

At last, he was home to stay.

2. John Adams

John Adams was born at 133 Franklin Street in Quincy, Massachusetts. He lived there until his marriage to Abigail Smith when they moved next door. The house at 141 Franklin Street now became his home and his law office and, in 1767, the birthplace of his son, John Quincy Adams, the sixth President. Mr. Adams was often away from home, becoming more active as one of the leaders of the thirteen colonies which would become the United States. His wife and son remained at home during the Revolutionary War. On June 17, 1775, Abigail and young John Quincy climbed the hill behind their house to watch a battle going on at Breed's Hill (which we call Bunker Hill) across the Charles River.

In 1783, the family went to Europe where Mr. Adams represented the new United States in the capitals of Europe. Four years later, the family came back and bought the old Borland place near their former home in Quincy. Mr. and Mrs. Adams hoped to retire there, and they began to call their new home "Peacefield."

But the house did not quite live up to their expectations. The rooms were tiny and the ceilings so low that Abigail Adams wrote to her daughter it felt "like a wren's house" and to "wear no feathers" when she came to visit.

Before they had a chance to begin any remodeling projects, Mr. Adams was called to New York to become the nation's first vice-president. Eight years later, he became the second

President of the United States, the first to live in Washington, D.C. and the White House.

Meanwhile, in Massachusetts, Mrs. Adams was managing the Adams home and farm as she had done for many years while her husband was away. She hired carpenters to make repairs on the house and then enlarge it, doubling its size. Much of it was completed without her husband's knowledge. Often he was surprised to come home and find that a new room, a new wing on the house or a complete new building had been added somewhere on the estate. A room which became a favorite was the second-floor study which Abigail Adams added to house her husband's growing library of books.

Finally, it seemed, Mr. Adams' public duties were over. After years of working to mold the thirteen colonies into one nation, John Adams went to Peacefield. There, he continued to live with his wife, until her death in 1818.

John Adams died in the upstairs study of Peacefield on July 4, 1826, exactly fifty years after he had voted for the Declaration of Independence. His last words were about his dear friend Thomas Jefferson. "Thomas Jefferson survives." Unknown to him, Jefferson had died just hours before at his estate in Virginia.

This is the home of both John Adams and John Quincy Adams, at 141 Franklin Street. Known as the "Old House," it was home to four generations of the Adams family. (National Park Service)

3. Thomas Jefferson

"Architecture is my delight," Thomas Jefferson wrote, "and putting up and pulling down one of my favorite amusements."

He began putting up his architectural masterpiece, Monticello, as a young lawyer of twenty-five, and did not stop putting up or pulling down some part of it until he died at eighty-three.

Jefferson had inherited the land near Charlottesville, Virginia, from his father, and soon he decided to build a house on a leveled area of a hill, an unheard of thing in those days. He named his home Monticello, meaning "little hill" in Italian. While studying at William and Mary College, he bought books on architecture and began to make plans.

Young Mr. Jefferson made dozens of drawings at first, but work on his new home moved slowly as he constantly changed them. He drew more and more designs, even those of the curtains that would hang at the windows. When his boyhood home, Shadwell, was destroyed by fire and he needed a place to live, he quickly completed the south pavilion of Monticello.

The south pavilion was only a one-room building, but it served as his bachelor quarters while the rest of the house was being built. Two years later, the bachelor quarters became the honeymoon cottage for his bride, Martha Shelton, and himself. Soon the main house was complete; it was about half the size it would become.

Mr. Jefferson had many unusual ideas he wanted to include

in the building of his home. For instance, he did not want the outbuildings such as the laundry and smokehouse to be seen, as they were at Mount Vernon. To hide them from view, he built two long terraces which flank the main house. Connecting the two terraces is an all-weather underground passageway in which he put many storage rooms for wine and grain. A kitchen, cook's room, servants' quarters and smoke room are hidden beneath the south terrace. The north terrace hides the stables, carriage house, ice house, and laundry.

Monticello, home of President Thomas Jefferson, at Charlottesville, Virginia. The President built this house from his own architectural designs. It has a number of modern features, some of which Jefferson himself invented. (Thomas Jefferson Memorial Foundation)

Mr. Jefferson's political career began in 1769, when he was elected to Virginia's legislature, called the House of Burgesses. Six years later, he traveled to Philadelphia to represent Virginia in the First Continental Congress. The following year it became his task to write down the reasons why the colonies should take up arms against England. The historic document he drafted was the Declaration of Independence, which took him two weeks to write. Of it he said, " . . . it was intended to be an expression of the American mind."

During the Revolutionary War, the British came to Monticello, hoping to capture Mr. Jefferson who was by then Governor of Virginia. He and his family narrowly escaped capture, having left only moments before. The British did no damage to the house and took only a few bottles of wine.

The war continued as Mr. Jefferson joined Benjamin Franklin and John Adams in Paris to help them make trade agreements with European countries. After they left, Thomas Jefferson became minister to France. During his five years in Europe, he studied the architecture and gardens of its grandest homes. When Mr. Jefferson returned to the United States, he brought with him eighty-six wooden crates in which he had packed such things as fifteen cases of books and forty-four chairs and sofas. He also had a head full of ideas that he wanted to use in remodeling Monticello.

Gradually the house took the form that we see today. It became a three-story building of thirty-five rooms, including twelve in the basement. Many rooms were necessary due to the number of people, including relatives and slaves, who lived at Monticello. Mr. Jefferson also enjoyed the company of his friends who were guests for weeks at a time.

Monticello is largely furnished with Mr. Jefferson's belongings, many of which were invented and designed by him for a particular purpose. Some of the devices exhibited are a seven-day calendar-clock and a dumbwaiter concealed in the mantel of the dining room fireplace. (A dumbwaiter is a small elevator pulled up and down by ropes. It was used to deliver food from the kitchen to the dining room upstairs.) Also on display are a replica of the small portable desk on which he probably wrote the Declaration of Independence, his special medicine chest, a revolving chair and worktable, a coffee urn, a pair of spectacles and many more items of special interest.

In 1819, he founded the University of Virginia. He designed many of its buildings, and made suggestions on subjects to be taught there.

He died on July 4, 1826, getting the wish he once had expressed to a friend, "All my wishes end where I hope my days will end. . . . at Monticello."

Jefferson's bedroom at Monticello. In keeping with the custom of the time, the bed occupies a private alcove within the bedroom.

4. James Madison

After he graduated from the College of New Jersey (now Princeton University), James Madison didn't know what to do with the rest of his life. For a while, he thought he wanted to be a minister. He also considered law and government. He went home to Montpelier, the family's thousand-acre plantation in Orange County, Virginia, to decide.

Soon he joined his father in organizing friends and neighbors into a group called "Committees of Correspondence." These groups were forming all over the colonies to protect citizens who had been wronged by British law.

James traveled from Montpelier to other parts of the state, writing, speaking and organizing against the British. Soon he met two other patriots who would share friendship as well as their futures with him, Thomas Jefferson and James Monroe.

Then in 1780, young Mr. Madison became a member of the Second Continental Congress, and he never again wondered about his choice of profession. He didn't return to Montpelier for two years, but when he did, his happy family gave many parties in his honor. After some weeks of helping his father supervise the work of the plantation, he returned to public life, governing the emerging nation.

Some years later, Mr. Madison thought that he wanted to retire to the privacy of Montpelier. With his wife, Dolley, he remodeled the already large house into an even larger mansion. He was helped by his friend, Thomas Jefferson, who made suggestions and, while in France, picked out a marble mantelpiece for the drawing room. James Monroe, the American representative to France, also sent gifts of table-cloths, napkins, chairs, couches and an iron bed from that country.

Together, the Madisons planted many trees in the garden which are still there. And under Mr. Madison's direction, farmhands cultivated corn and tobacco which became the paying crops of the estate.

Dolley Madison soon acquired a deserved reputation as the most popular hostess of her day. She turned Montpelier and later, the White House, into the scene of many exciting parties and lavish dinners.

After his two terms of office were completed, Mr. Madison and his wife retired permanently to Montpelier. Now he found time to work on his collection of books in the library, and Dolley continued to entertain at magnificent dinners. In order to keep fresh food on hand for her parties, the ex-President built the first icebox in Virginia.

After the Madisons' death, Montpelier was sold to pay their debts. Now privately owned, the estate, except for the Madison family cemetery, is not open to the public.

The gardens at Montpelier, the home of James and Dolley Madison, in Orange County, Virginia. (Virginia Conservation Commission)

5. James Monroe

In 1795, when James Monroe began to plan his home, which he called "Highlands," he was in France representing the United States. However, his friend, Thomas Jefferson, agreed to oversee the construction. He had long encouraged James and Elizabeth Monroe to become his neighbors in Albemarle County, Virginia.

The two men had been close friends since James Monroe studied law in Jefferson's offices. Then Mr. Monroe followed his friend and teacher into public life, serving their new nation. Soon they became closely linked with another Virginian and neighbor, James Madison.

The Monroes moved into the almost completed Highlands, two-and-one-half miles from Monticello, on November 23, 1799. If the elegant furniture they brought home from France seemed out of place in the small, country home, the Monroes were not concerned. They settled down in their "cabin-castle," a nickname Mr. Monroe gave it, and began to entertain their friends. Thomas Jefferson came often. So did James and Dolley Madison.

Because he had little money to support his family, Mr. Monroe also tried farming, hoping he would have a profitable plantation.

But soon he was called away once again, to represent the United States in Europe and then to become Secretary of State when James Madison was President. Finally, he became President himself in 1817. Highlands, both house and land,

Ashlawn, home of President Monroe, at Charlottesville, Virginia. It is a simple two-story, white frame dwelling typical of many farm houses of the area. Ashlawn is noted for its boxwood garden, designed after gardens which the President had seen in France when he was a diplomat there. Jefferson's Monticello is only about two miles down the road from Ashlawn. (Virginia State Travel Service)

had no one to manage it after the Monroes left, and it soon fell apart.

After the Monroes sold Highlands in 1826, several other families owned it, changed its name to Ash Lawn and added another story to the house. In 1974, Ash Lawn was given to the College of William and Mary, the university which James Monroe and Thomas Jefferson attended. The College restored the house to look as it did when the Monroes had lived there. Once again, the living room, dining room, nursery, study, two bedrooms and basement kitchen are furnished to give the feeling of a working country home. Local spinners, a blacksmith and other craftsmen work on the estate and demonstrate colonial skills to visitors.

The boxwood gardens were not added until after the Monroe family left Ash Lawn. But the statue of James Monroe in the center of the gardens reminds visitors whose home this once was.

While Mr. Monroe was President, he began to build a much larger home near Washington, D.C. He planted an oak for each state in the Union on the property, giving the estate its name, Oak Hill. He retired to Oak Hill after he left the White House, but had to sell it to pay his many debts. It is privately owned and not open to the public.

He lived his last year in his daughter's New York home and died on July 4, 1831, five years to the day after his good friend, Thomas Jefferson. He is buried at Oak Hill.

6. John Quincy Adams

John Quincy Adams served his country nearly all his life. When he was only fourteen, he was appointed secretary to Francis Dana, the first American ambassador to Russia. Because John Quincy spoke French very well, a language he learned while going to school in Paris, he was asked to become the official interpreter for Mr. Dana. French was the language of diplomats in Russia. John Quincy returned to the United States when he was eighteen, and finished his education at Harvard University.

After he married Louisa Johnson, he brought her home to Peacefield. But they didn't stay long. Young Mr. Adams became the minister to Russia and then to England. Now he represented the United States as his father once had done, and helped to arrange treaties with other countries. The most important one was the Treaty of Ghent which ended the War of 1812 with Great Britain.

When James Monroe became President, he asked young Mr. Adams to become his Secretary of State. Eight years later, much to his father's delight, John Quincy Adams became the sixth President of the United States.

After his one term, Mr. Adams returned to Peacefield where he hoped to withdraw from public life. Since the death of his parents, the house and gardens had been neglected, so he immediately began to repair and rebuild them. First, he added a long passageway to connect both sides of the large house. Then he planted many trees on the estate. During the summers, he worked in the fields with the hired hands.

Two years later, he was asked to represent the Plymouth, Massachusetts, Congressional district and accepted. He became the only former President to serve in the House of Representatives and remained for nine consecutive terms.

Mr. Adams became too busy in Washington to pay much attention to Peacefield, so he turned the job over to his son, Charles Francis. Charles tore down old buildings, improved the kitchen and built a library made of stone. In it he placed the family's most prized possessions: their books and papers.

The story of Peacefield did not end with Charles Francis Adams. His four sons continued to give it loving care while also using the Stone Library to further their careers as writers, historians and politicians. In 1927, when the youngest son died, the great old house was given to the Adams Memorial Society and later to the American people.

The library of the "Old House" at Quincy, Massachusetts contains books and papers which belong to both Presidents, John Adams and John Quincy Adams, who lived there. (National Park Service)

7. Andrew Jackson

When Andrew Jackson purchased twelve hundred acres in western Tennessee in 1804, he decided it was time to settle down and work the land. Already he had been the state's first representative in the U.S. Congress, senator and judge of the Superior Court. He was an officer in the state militia, too.

He named his land The Hermitage, and planted one thousand apple and peach trees as well as cotton and corn. For many years, Mr. Jackson and his wife, Rachel, lived in one of the log cabins on the property while they farmed and entertained visitors such as President Monroe and Aaron Burr, who was Vice-President under Thomas Jefferson.

From time to time, Mr. Jackson left Tennessee to fight in major battles. He commanded the Tennessee militia in the Creek Indian uprising in Alabama. During the War of 1812, he fought the Indians at the Battle of Horseshoe Bend, receiving the rank of major general. And with his defeat of the British in the Battle of New Orleans, he became a national hero.

Now the Jacksons decided to build a very large home, which would also be called The Hermitage. It is thought that General Jackson designed it and had his slaves build it from material found on his land. The foundation was made of native limestone. Bricks for the walls came from clay in the fields, and roofs, flooring and beams were cut from poplar and cedar trees in their woods. A beautiful garden was planted and lovingly taken care of by Rachel Jackson. Soon

The back parlor at the Hermitage, home of President Andrew Jackson, near Nashville, Tennessee. The Hermitage is a typical southern plantation home. This room contains the original Empire style furniture and the expensive Brussells carpets. (Ladies' Hermitage Association)

the mansion became the center of many happy gatherings for the Jacksons and their friends.

In 1824, the Marquis de Lafayette came to The Hermitage. He was a French nobleman who had helped the United States during the Revolutionary War. After dinner, General Jackson showed him a pair of pistols which the Marquis had given George Washington in 1778. They had been given to General Jackson after President Washington's death. The Marquis said that he was happy to find the pistols in such worthy hands.

Jackson became President in the election of 1828, beginning a period called the "Age of the Common Man." Because he was the first President who did not come from a rich Virginia or Massachusetts family, Jackson felt he represented the common, or ordinary, citizens.

While away in Washington, his thoughts were often on The Hermitage, and he sent back instructions for remodeling it. After the work was finished, fire nearly destroyed the house in 1834. The mansion was rebuilt, keeping the old brick walls which were painted white to hide the smoke stains. When it was finished once more, President Jackson ordered furniture that can still be seen there today. In his orders, the President requested only that the bedposts be plain, so they would be easy to dust.

After two terms of office, President Jackson returned to The Hermitage. There he lived out his days as an elder statesman in the home he had built and loved for many years.

President Andrew Jackson's bedroom at the Hermitage. This bedroom and the back parlor seen in the previous picture help to show why the Hermitage was regarded as the most luxurious home in Tennessee before the Civil War. (Ladies' Hermitage Association)

8. Martin Van Buren

"What curious creatures we are." That was Martin Van Buren's comment about the many changes previous owners had made on the fine old house he purchased in 1839. He was already President when he bought Lindenwald, in his home town of Kinderhook, near the Hudson River in New York State. After he was defeated for a second term, he moved to Lindenwald to decide what to do with the rest of his life.

He had held political offices since he was a young man. Before becoming President, he had been county surrogate, state senator, state attorney general, U.S. senator, governor of New York, Secretary of State, minister to Great Britain and then Vice-President.

After some thought, he made up his mind. There was no need to change careers. He would continue in politics and try to win the Presidency again.

Having noticed that other Presidential homes had become national shrines and attractions to the public, he decided to turn Lindenwald into such an estate, too. Perhaps such a setting would rally voters around him once again.

Now he, too, began to make changes at Lindenwald. Mr. Van Buren called in an architect to enlarge the house which already included a forty-two-foot-long ballroom. Two new kitchens were added as well as a library wing and a four-story tower with ninety-nine steps. The central hall was used as a banquet room and contained a table which could seat sixty-five guests. A furnace was installed in the basement which heated the entire house. The central heating was considered a new-fangled curiosity, and so were the indoor bathrooms which he also added.

Mr. Van Buren had many distinguished guests visit his thirty-six room house. Washington Irving who wrote "The Legend of Sleepy Hollow" was one guest, Kentucky's Senator Henry Clay another. But there were no crowds clamoring for his return to the Presidency. After his defeat by General Zachary Taylor in 1848, Mr. Van Buren retired from public life.

He lived alone at Lindenwald for many years. His wife had died years before, and his four sons were grown. Then his youngest son, his wife, and their children moved in to keep the ex-President company during his last years.

After Mr. Van Buren's death in 1862, the house and its furnishings were sold. Over the years, the various owners made many more changes to the house. Recently acquired by the National Park Service, the house is being changed again. This time, however, the change will be a return to the way it looked during the days when Martin Van Buren lived there.

Lindenwald, home of President Martin Van Buren, at Kinderhook, New York. It is the home Van Buren owned when he was elected President, and is the place where he died at the age of 79.

(National Park Service)

9. William Henry Harrison

Like President Jackson, William Henry Harrison was a frontier general, but he was born in a Virginia mansion called "Berkeley" rather than a backwoods log cabin. Berkeley was a beautiful brick house surrounded by acres of woodlands which had been the home of Harrisons for generations. William was old enough to remember the day in 1781 when he fled Berkeley with his family just before the British came. Led by a colonist, Benedict Arnold who had become a traitor, the Red Coats burned and raided the mansion, stealing furnishings and servants. It was several years before the Harrisons could restore the mansion and live there again.

After his father died, William turned to a military career which took him to the Northwest Territory, the land between the Ohio River and Great Lakes. He served there until he resigned to become governor general of Indiana Territory.

This was not an easy office to fill. It was Governor Harrison's duty to make the frontier safe from attacks by angry Indians who felt their land had been taken from them unfairly and given to white settlers. Governor Harrison also had the job of organizing a territorial government.

Arriving in Vincennes, the capital of Indiana Territory in 1801, Governor Harrison bought three hundred acres which he called Grouseland. During the next several years, he built a 26-room brick mansion which looked much like Berkeley, the Harrison mansion in Virginia. There were certain differences, however. Berkeley was not built to withstand Indian attack. Grouseland was.

Berkeley Plantation, the ancestral home of the Harrison family, two of whom became President. However, Benjamin Harrison never lived here —it was the home of his grandfather, William Henry Harrison, the ninth President. (Virginia State Travel Service)

Two false windows in the front wall of the Grouseland house and lookout peepholes in the attic for sharpshooters gave the Harrison family some protection. For emergency escapes in case of attack, there was a trapdoor on the second floor which lead to the first floor and an underground passage leading to another building. A powder magazine for ammunition and a basement well for water were ready if the house came under attack for many days.

Perhaps the time of most worry at Grouseland occurred when Tecumseh, Chief of the Shawnee tribe arrived with four hundred warriors to talk. A company of soldiers positioned inside the house waited for any sign of trouble as the talks went on outside. There was no bloodshed at this time, but in 1811, when General Harrison and the Indian chieftain fought in a battle on the Tippecanoe River, Tecumseh was beaten.

General Harrison ran for the presidency in 1840, using the slogan, "Tippecanoe and Tyler, too" and won. Already old, tired and ill, President Harrison lived only one month after taking office, presiding over the shortest term in our nation's history.

10. John Tyler

His opponents called him "His Accidency," and felt that he should be only an Acting President after William Henry Harrison died. There was no precedent for John Tyler to follow, since he was the first Vice-President to succeed to the Presidency following the death of the President in office. Tyler had his own ideas about running the country, and followed them rather than those of Congress. This independence won him more political enemies than friends. For this reason, he thought of himself as a political outlaw.

After he left the White House, President Tyler returned to his estate along the James River in Charles City County, Virginia. He bought an estate in 1842, and renamed it "Sherwood Forest," after Robin Hood's hideout. Robin Hood was a famous outlaw in English literature.

The house was a two-and-a-half-story structure of clapboard which President Tyler began to remodel and enlarge to fit his growing family of fourteen children. He connected the detached kitchen to the rest of the house, and added a ballroom on the west end. The length of a football field, it is considered the longest framehouse in the United States.

President and Mrs. Tyler enjoyed their years in retirement at Sherwood Forest. They entertained with dinners and dances in the sixty-eight-foot-long ballroom which Mrs. Tyler designed for Virginia reels. To dance a reel, couples needed plenty of space. Facing each other in a long line, they skipped or danced with one another in figure-eight patterns up and down the dance floor.

Sherwood Forest, home of President John Tyler. It is one room deep and 300 feet long—one of the longest of all private homes in the United States. (Virginia State Travel Service)

The Tylers also invited friends to visit them in their sitting room, called the "Gray Room" by the family. It is said that the room has been occupied for two hundred years by the ghost of Mrs. Gray, a former nursemaid who comes down a hidden staircase each night. Then she settles down and rocks until dawn, in a rocking chair that isn't there!

When trouble began between the North and the South, which later ended in the Civil War, the ex-President tried to keep the peace. His efforts did not help and, at last, he sided with the Confederacy, becoming a member of the Confederate Congress. He died in January, 1862 while attending a meeting in Richmond.

Union troops occupied the estate during the war. They cut down many trees for firewood and damaged the house and its belongings. Cracks in the front door made by their rifles, and burns and rifle shots on the books in the sitting room can still be seen.

Today, the house is owned and has been restored by Mr. and Mrs. Harrison R. Tyler. Mr. Tyler is the youngest grandson of the President.

11. James K. Polk

By the time James Polk came to the White House as the eleventh President in 1845, he had been in politics for a long time. Mr. Polk was a member of the House of Representatives, having served Tennessee for fourteen years. During that time, he was twice elected Speaker of the House.

He was also known as Andrew Jackson's friend, the man who would speak out for President Jackson's policies in Congress. Later, in Mr. Jackson's Tennessee home, a group of friends nominated Mr. Polk for President.

Yet, when elected, President Polk said, "I intend to be *myself*, President of the United States."

He was just that. President Polk set himself four goals and accomplished all of them during the one term he said he would serve. One of these was expanding the territory of the country. He added over 800,000 square miles—the southwest territories and California—after a war with Mexico to settle ownership. He avoided a war with Great Britain by getting a peaceful agreement on the boundary between the American northwest and British Canada.

President Polk had bought a large home for his retirement days when he returned to Tennessee. But he lived only three months in the house, and it was later destroyed after his wife's death.

Today, tourists visit the brick home built by his father in Columbia, Tennessee in 1816, while James was away at college. The future President lived here for a time after his graduation and before he left to begin his career in law and politics.

Most of the furnishings now at this home were used by the President and his wife in the White House and his law office. Several items from his inaugural are there, including the Bible on which he took his oath of office and a beautiful fan which Mrs. Polk carried to the inaugural ball. President Polk had it designed to show pictures of the first eleven presidents and of the signing of the Declaration of Independence.

Pieces from the china, silver and crystal used for White House state dinners are on display as well as original early drawings of the Washington Monument in Washington, D.C. President Polk laid the cornerstone for it during his term of office.

One of the most unusual pieces in the Polk home is a colored marble table in the parlor. The eagle design on it is made with many small pieces of stone. The eagle is surrounded by thirty stars, representing each of the states in the newly expanded country. It is also a reminder of the man who is now known as the only President to have met all his goals and, for that reason, is considered by historians as one of our greatest Presidents.

The parlor of the James K. Polk home, called Polk Place, in Nashville, Tennessee. The French gilt candelabrum (a candlestick having several arms or branches) beneath the painting of Mrs. Polk was used in the White House. Visitors can still see the table with the eagle design. (Jesse F. Foreman)

12. Zachary Taylor

He was only a baby in 1785 when his parents moved to a farm about five miles east of what was then the village of Louisville, Kentucky. At first, the family lived in a small, twelve-foot-square cabin. In a few years, Zachary's father had become successful at farming. Now he began to build a much larger brick house which had two-and-a-half-stories and a basement. Each of the eight rooms had a fireplace. Walnut paneling in the entrance hallway and dining room, plus door locks and real window glass gave the home a prosperous look.

The family farmed the four hundred acres which surrounded the house, and Zachary soon learned to be ready for anything on the frontier. He learned to ride, shoot, hunt, and farm the rich soil, while watching out for hostile Indians. His formal schooling was limited, and he never did learn to spell correctly.

Zachary lived in his boyhood home, called "Springfield," until he joined the Army at the age of twenty-three. Two years later, he returned home to be married there.

The young lieutenant rose to the rank of general, and rode to victory and fame during the Mexican War, which settled the ownership of California and the southwest. Even after the war, the picture of "Rough and Ready" Taylor astride his horse, Old Whitey, inspired many soldiers to remember him as hero and leader.

After many years of serving at military posts and never having a permanent home, General Taylor retired. He returned to farming, an occupation he learned to love during his early years at Springfield.

But he was still a national hero, and many politicians wanted him to run for the Presidency because they knew he would be popular with the voters. He was also a slave-owner which would make him a vote getter in the South. Although he said he disliked politics and had never even voted in a Presidential election, he was easily elected.

He didn't stay there long. Just sixteen months in office, he became ill on the Fourth of July, while attending a ceremony at the Washington Monument. He died a few days later.

Springfield passed out of Taylor family ownership many years ago. Changes have been made to the house by several owners and also by nature, in 1974, when a tornado severely damaged the house. Not open to the public at the present time, it is currently being restored by the owners.

13. Millard Fillmore

When Millard Fillmore was eighteen years old, he finally had enough money to buy a book for the first time. It was a dictionary. He also met Abigail Powers, a schoolteacher. After that, his education improved rapidly. He read the book and married the schoolteacher. Five years later, he became a lawyer and began to practice law in Buffalo, New York.

Soon he entered politics. He represented his district in the New York State legislature before being elected to the House of Representatives where he served for four terms.

In 1848, he was selected to be Zachary Taylor's running mate, providing a contrast to the rough and ready general. Fillmore was a northerner, while Taylor came from the south. He had experience in government and politics, Taylor had none.

After President Taylor's death in 1850, Millard Fillmore became President and helped to pass the Compromise of 1850 in Congress. The Compromise was a series of bills to prevent the spread of slavery. They were designed to please both the northern and southern states. The Compromise admitted California as a free state, and Utah and New Mexico became territories. It also settled a dispute between Texas and New Mexico, stopped slave trade in the District of Columbia, and created a strong fugitive slave law.

For his retirement years, Mr. Fillmore bought a large mansion in Buffalo, but Mrs. Fillmore was never to live there. Before they could return from Washington, she caught a cold and died. Some years later, Mr. Fillmore remarried and enjoyed an active life as Buffalo's leading citizen. His home became the scene of many civic and social affairs.

Only once did the townspeople become upset with Mr. Fillmore. When President Lincoln died, the people agreed to drape their homes in black to show their respect, a custom of the times. Someone in Mr. Fillmore's family was ill, so he did not hear of the plans. When the citizens noticed that his house was not draped in black, they threw bottles of ink at his home, staining the walls.

After Mr. Fillmore's death, the large house and all his possessions were sold. His papers, letters and journals were burned by his son. Later, the mansion was torn down, too, giving historians little to examine in telling Mr. Fillmore's story.

One link to Mr. Fillmore's life remains. A home in which he lived briefly in East Aurora, New York still exists. However, it has been moved and remodeled so many times that it is doubtful if even Millard Fillmore would recognize it today.

14. Franklin Pierce

When Franklin Pierce became President in 1853, the northern and southern states of the nation already were quarreling over slavery and secession. However, President Pierce was a man of peace. He felt the nation should be wise enough to settle its family troubles by compromise, and he devoted his term of office to avoiding a civil war.

It was not unusual for him to think of the country as a family, and its problems as a family quarrel. He had grown up in Hillsboro, New Hampshire, in a large family to whom feelings of harmony and love were important.

His father came to Hillsboro shortly after the Revolutionary War, purchased some land and married. He lived in a log cabin with his wife and children, until he began to build the house now known as the Homestead. He completed it in 1804, the year Franklin was born.

The large, white frame house became the center of all family activities and the town's as well. Besides the parents, eight children and thirteen servants, the townspeople often were present. Dances in the ballroom, political meetings in the parlor and a tavern in the house run by Franklin's father provided everyone with all of the excitement and recreation they could want.

When Franklin was fourteen, he went away to school, but looked forward to his return to Hillsboro for each vacation.

One time when he came home, he found his father drilling the local militia in the ballroom. Another time he returned to find the mansion had been redecorated with more elegant furniture and expensive scenic wallpaper from Italy. The grounds also had been improved with gardens, a summer house and a pond for fishing.

Franklin entered Bowdoin College at Brunswick, Maine, in 1820, with classmates such as Henry Wadsworth Longfellow, Calvin Ellis Stowe and Nathaniel Hawthorne all of whom would one day become as famous as he. (Longfellow became a poet, Hawthorne an author and poet, and Stowe a minister who married Harriet Beecher Stowe, author of *Uncle Tom's Cabin.*) After graduating, he studied law and returned to Hillsboro to open an office across the road from the Homestead. He continued to live at home until his marriage in 1834.

Although Franklin never lived in the family home again, he returned there from time to time for inspiration. When he was elected to the Presidency, he returned once more, to pray at the graves of his parents and prepare his mind for leading a national family through troubled times.

The Homestead remained in the Pierce family until 1925, when it was given to the state of New Hampshire. It has been restored to its appearance at the time of Franklin Pierce's earliest and happiest years as a member of a large, family whose hospitality recognized no boundaries.

15. James Buchanan

When James Buchanan bought his Pennsylvania country home called "Wheatland" in 1848, it soon became the scene of many political meetings and social gatherings. During those pre-Civil War years, leaders of the North and South came there for his advice. Already a proven leader, he had served his country for many years in the House, Senate, President Polk's cabinet and as a diplomat.

Mr. Buchanan was a good host to his friends who visited at Wheatland. Guests were picked up at the railroad station in Lancaster, Pennsylvania, and taken by horse and carriage to the seventeen-room brick house on the edge of town. Overlooking a gentle slope of lawn and flanked by tree lined driveways, Wheatland was the perfect setting for furthering Mr. Buchanan's presidential ambitions.

Sometimes the portly host waited on the front portico to welcome his guests. When it was time for dinner, he greeted each one as he or she entered the dining room. Dinner was served at the table especially built for the room, and which never has been removed from the house. When the table is pulled out to full length, it can seat twenty-six people for a state dinner.

After dessert, everyone moved into the front parlor with its marble fireplace, crystal chandelier and signed portraits of the British Queen Victoria and her husband, Prince Albert.

Mr. Buchanan's niece, Harriet Lane, often entertained by playing the Chickering grand piano. She acted as her uncle's official hostess at Wheatland, at Queen Victoria's court in England and later at the White House.

In June, 1856, Mr. Buchanan received the news that he had been nominated for the Presidency at last. During the campaign, Wheatland became a symbol. In many parts of the country, his supporters formed "Wheatland Clubs" to promote his election.

The following March, he left Wheatland for Washington escorted to the railroad station by bands and cheering citizens. However, his one term was not a happy one, as he tried in vain to settle the differences between the North and South.

Mr. Buchanan never married. He returned to Wheatland in 1861 and continued the improvements on his house begun earlier. In 1850, he had installed a furnace and cast-iron kitchen range to replace the open hearth in the basement. After his return, he ordered a new-fangled icebox, although he worried that he would not be able to find ice for it in the summer time. Perhaps the installation that caused the most stir among his guests was the paneled bathroom. The deep zinc-lined tub was considered a luxury in the 1850s, although it could only be filled by carrying water to it. There was no plumbing in those days.

President Buchanan died at Wheatland in 1868. Few changes have been made to the house since then.

16. Abraham Lincoln

Nearly everyone knows that Abraham Lincoln was born in a log cabin. After he moved from that cabin, he lived in many other places before he stepped into the White House, fifty-two years later. However, of all the homes he lived in, he owned only one. That was the house at the corner of Eighth and Jackson streets in Springfield, Illinois.

After Abraham Lincoln and Mary Todd were married in 1842, they moved into some furnished rooms at the Globe Tavern. (Hotels often were called taverns in those days.) When their first child, Robert, was born a year later, they knew they would need more room in which to live. And so they bought their first and only house.

The boyhood home of Abraham Lincoln, at Dale, Indiana. This one-room cabin looks pretty crude, but it is not nearly as crude as the cabin Lincoln was born in, near Hogdenville, Kentucky.

Mr. Lincoln paid fifteen hundred dollars for it, a year's salary in 1844, but it was thought to be a good investment. The house was well built and had been well cared for. The previous owners had painted it light brown with dark green shutters, and this pleased the Lincolns.

But like most new homeowners, they began to make improvements of their own. Mr. Lincoln built a two-foot-high brick wall in front of the house, and he also designed a front yard iron fence which still stands today. When Mrs. Lincoln inherited some money, they added a second story to give them more room for their growing family.

Mrs. Lincoln liked to entertain guests in her new house, and persuaded her husband to put on his best broadcloth suit so that he would look presentable. Mr. Lincoln enjoyed visitors, too, but his favorite times seemed to be those spent in the company of his family, alone. Many evenings after supper, he stretched out on the living room carpet and read while his young sons played around him.

This drab looking town house in Springfield, Illinois was the only house Lincoln ever owned. In the photo are Mr. Lincoln and his boys, Tad and Willie. The picture was taken in 1860, at about the time Lincoln became a presidential candidate. (Louis A. Warren Lincoln Library and Museum, Fort Wayne, Indiana)

When Mr. Lincoln was nominated for the Presidency in May, 1860, brass bands and crowds of neighbors serenaded the family. Mr. Lincoln stepped outside the front door, and said he wished his house was big enough to ask all of them to come inside. In February, 1861, when Mr. Lincoln and his family left for Washington, he said goodbye at the railroad station. "I now leave, not knowing when or whether ever I may return." He never did. He was shot on April 14, 1865 and died the next morning.

Few changes have been made inside the house at Eighth and Jackson since the Lincolns lived there. The wallpaper Mrs. Lincoln selected is still on the walls. Mr. Lincoln's favorite rocking chair is in a corner of the parlor near Tad's wicker-back chair. A world globe stands beside the bookcase which Mr. Lincoln used as a desk. His stovepipe hat hangs in the hall, and his children's toys clutter a small bedroom.

Thousands of visitors come each year to the house at Eighth and Jackson, expecting to tour a shrine. They leave with the feeling that they have just visited friends.

Friends and neighbors gathered in front of Lincoln's Springfield, Illinois home to show him their support in his presidential campaign.
(Louis A. Warren Lincoln Library and Museum, Fort Wayne, Indiana)

17. Andrew Johnson

By the time he was eighteen years old, Andrew Johnson was already married and established as a tailor in Greeneville, Tennessee. With his wife, he settled in a two-room house on Main Street. He used one room as a shop and lived in the other. Because he had never gone to school, his wife helped him learn to read and write. Soon his tailor shop became the center of village politics, and Johnson employed others to read to him as he worked so that he would know what was happening in the states. Now his business began to prosper, and Johnson, his wife and children moved to a larger home. He moved his tailor shop to a new and separate location, also.

When he was twenty-one, the townspeople elected him alderman, and two years later, he was mayor. From mayor he moved quickly to state representative. In 1843, the year he won election to the U.S. House of Representatives, he hired someone to take care of his tailor shop. He had little time for it now, and even less when he became governor of Tennessee and then its U.S. senator.

Mr. Johnson considered himself a southerner and he was a slaveholder. But he did not believe a slave state should leave, or secede, from the Union. In 1860, he delivered a speech in Congress in which he said, "I stand by the Constitution as it is . . . it is the last hope of human freedom."

In the election of 1864, when President Lincoln was looking for a running mate, he remembered Senator Johnson's strong feelings about the Constitution and recommended him to the convention delegates. They agreed, and Johnson became Vice-President. He became President the following year when President Lincoln was assassinated.

President Johnson tried to carry out Mr. Lincoln's postwar program. He hoped to bring the southern states back into the union as quickly as possible and re-unite the country in a spirit of harmony. But many congressmen felt the southern states should be punished. The President disagreed with Congress. Eventually this conflict led to his impeachment. After a long trial, he was found innocent and finished his term.

President Johnson finally returned to Greeneville, and the house he called home but had not found time to live in for many years. While still a representative, he had bought another, more stately, two-story brick house on Main Street. From time to time, the Johnsons added rooms, porches and even a wing to the house, looking forward to their retirement.

During the Civil War, both Confederate and Federal soldiers occupied the house. When the Johnsons returned home, they found names of men and companies as well as words of advice written on the walls. One comment began, "Andy, you had better skedaddle . . ."

Descendants of President Johnson owned the house and lived in it until it was purchased by the government in 1942. As a result, every room has furnishings either used by the Johnsons or having a direct connection with the family. All of Mr. Johnson's papers, books, dishes and other household belongings are there, together with gifts given him while he was President. Two favorites of visitors are a table with a tilt-top which is made of five hundred pieces of inlaid wood presented by the people of Ireland, and a hand-carved ivory basket presented by Queen Emma of the Hawaiian Islands.

Home of President Andrew Johnson, at Greeneville, Tennessee. The house is far better than the place where, at the age of 18, Mr. Johnson set up his tailor shop. Both houses still stand, and are part of the Andrew Johnson National Historic Site, established in 1942. (National Park Service)

18. Ulysses S. Grant

His mother called him "Lyss" when he was a boy. Others called him "Useless" as he grew up, because he never seemed to do anything quite right. When he was seventeen, Ulysses was accepted at West Point Military Academy, and was afraid that someone there would notice his initials, H.U.G. He had been given the name, Hiram Ulysses Grant, at birth.

But through a mistake in his appointment papers, he was admitted as Ulysses Simpson Grant. Someone nicknamed him Uncle Sam when they saw his name written as U.S. Grant. He didn't bother to change it back to Hiram.

His career in the Army didn't last long. After serving during the Mexican War, he resigned with the rank of captain to try farming and several other jobs. But Captain Grant was unsuccessful in whatever he tried to do. So he took his family to Galena, Illinois, to clerk in his father's store.

When the Civil War began in 1861, there was a call for troops by President Lincoln. Captain Grant returned to the Army immediately and soon began winning battles for the North. Now he earned a new nickname when newspapers began to call him Unconditional Surrender Grant. In battles that he won for the North, he usually demanded unconditional surrender by the southern troops. His popularity grew as his military leadership brought the war to an end.

After a triumphant tour of the North, General Grant returned to Galena with his family. He was greeted by a crowd of over ten thousand people. A grand celebration

The kitchen (top) and library-office (bottom) in the Galena, Illinois home of President Ulysses S. Grant.
(State of Illinois Department of Conservation)

The parlor in President Grant's home. The handsome furniture was made of heavy, ornately carved wood. He left this home to become President.

followed which included parades, fireworks, speeches, and a reception ball. During the ceremonies, the citizens of Galena presented the General and his family with a completely furnished house on Bouthillier Street. It is said that when Grant completed his inspection of the house, he walked out on its front porch with tears glistening on his cheeks.

The General and Mrs. Grant did not live in the house very long. Although they liked the solid brick structure with its beautiful ornate furnishings, Galena was too far from Washington. They returned once in awhile to stay on Bouthillier Street for short periods.

General Grant never had been interested in politics, but his popularity and his position as commanding general of the Army kept him in the public eye. He couldn't avoid being nominated for the Presidency in 1868. That fall, the Grants returned to Galena and remained there while he conducted his successful campaign.

When General Grant left Galena once again, he had a new name—President.

The house presented to General Grant by the grateful people of Galena, as a reward for his outstanding service in the Civil War. (State of Illinois, Department of Conservation)

General Grant standing on the front porch of his home about 1865.
(The boy is not identified.) Unfortunately, Grant's later life was very
tragic. After retiring as President, he was financially ruined in an
investment mistake, and then became gravely ill. Despite this,
however, Grant was able to write his memoirs, while living in and
around New York City. (Chicago Historical Society)

19. Rutherford B. Hayes

The twenty-five acre estate in Fremont, Ohio, that once belonged to Rutherford B. Hayes is a peaceful place. Deep woods surround the large house. After rains, pools of clear standing water reflected the woods' giant oaks like mirrors. An uncle of Mr. Hayes named the land "Spiegel Grove" because the area reminded him of German fairy tales of long ago. (*Spiegel* is the word for mirror in German.)

According to history, the land once belonged to the Huron Indians who used a trail which followed a natural water highway from the Great Lakes to the Gulf of Mexico. A half-mile portion of this trail crosses Spiegel Grove. Explorers and missionaries followed it. So did French and British settlers. It was used by soldiers in the Revolutionary War. During the War of 1812, General William Henry Harrison converted it into a military road. After being captured by the Indians, Daniel Boone walked it as their prisoner.

Today, behind heavy iron gates which once ringed the White House, the Spiegel Grove estate includes the large twenty-bedroom home, the library and museum, and the President's tomb. The library and museum house over 80,000 books and 1,000,000 manuscripts. All the details are there concerning President Hayes' long career in public life as a general in the Civil War, as U.S. representative in Congress and governor of Ohio. Then he won the Presidency in one of the closest elections in the nation's history—by only one electoral vote.

While the family lived in the White House, the President's daughter, Fanny, played with a collection of doll houses. These are now on display in the museum at Spiegel Grove, as well as some of the fancy dresses her mother wore as First Lady.

In 1877, President Hayes' first year in office, he began a custom of naming trees in Spiegel Grove for distinguished guests who came to visit. Some of the famous names acquired by the trees include William McKinley, James A. Garfield, and Grover Cleveland—all presidents of the United States—and William T. Sherman, northern Army general during the Civil War.

Even after the President's death in 1893, the custom continued. President William Howard Taft selected for his name-tree one of the grandest oaks in the grove which grew directly in front of the mansion. Placing his hand upon it, he said, "This is about my size." President Taft weighed over three hundred pounds.

20. James A. Garfield

James A. Garfield was the last of our presidents who was born in a log cabin. After his father died, young James helped his mother and brothers and sisters run the small Ohio farm on which the cabin was located. Even with all his chores, he found time to read and study hard. Soon he went on to college, and graduated from Williams College in Massachusetts. Shortly after he began to teach in Hiram, Ohio, he married Lucretia Rudolph, a childhood friend.

The young man served as an Ohio senator, but resigned to enter the Army after the Civil War began. While he was fighting for the North, the people of Ohio elected him to serve in the House of Representatives. Major General Garfield resigned once more, this time from the Army, and went to the capitol immediately. He would be re-elected eight times.

When he returned to Ohio to campaign in the election of 1876, Congressman Garfield happened to see a farm near Mentor, Ohio, which was for sale. He bought it immediately because it reminded him of the farm he had lived on as a boy. It was also a place "Where my boys can learn to work and where I can touch the earth and get some strength from it." He and his wife were the parents of five boys and one girl.

The Garfields enlarged the farmhouse, which they called "Lawnfield," to a two-and-a-half story structure, with a wide-open porch across the front. If Mr. Garfield was the last of the log cabin presidents, he was also the first to conduct a "front-porch campaign" for the Presidency. Because he gave so many speeches from his porch or garden or living room, the campaign soon became known as a front-porch campaign.

Although Mr. Garfield had been nominated, he traveled very little during the spring and summer of 1880. Yet his popularity grew and visitors flocked to see him. The Lake Shore and Michigan Southern Railroad ran special tracks that crossed his farm, with a special stop arranged near the cow-path leading to the house. Campaign headquarters, located in a small building nearby, was fully equipped with a telegraph key that gave Mr. Garfield the latest news from around the country. It was here that he learned he had been elected President.

His term was a short one. President Garfield was shot on July 2, 1881 and died of an infection in the wound two months later.

Lawnfield, home of President James A. Garfield, at Mentor, Ohio, near Lake Erie. The house is not far from where President Garfield was born, but his birthplace was a pioneer's log cabin.

21. Chester A. Arthur

Chester A. Arthur was one of two Presidents who were born in Vermont. The other was Calvin Coolidge. Both of them came to the Presidency through the death of their predecessor.

Chester Arthur's life began on October 5, 1830 in a small cottage near North Fairfield. His education was supervised by his father, a minister and teacher, who saw to it that his son attended good schools. By the time Chester was eighteen, he had graduated from Union College and began teaching in a nearby town.

When Chester was twenty-three, he moved to New York to study law. Again, he was an excellent student and quickly became a skillful, wealthy attorney.

He married in 1859, and later bought a home at 123 Lexington Avenue in New York City. From this home, he began his political career, and quickly earned a reputation as a strong, capable leader. He was nominated to the Vice-Presidency in 1880, and succeeded to the highest office when President Garfield died. He took the oath of office in his New York home to become the 21st President of the United States.

The Arthur home in New York, a five-story brownstone, has changed through the years. The original entrance has disappeared, and a store now occupies the first floor. Nothing remains that once belonged to President Arthur, and it is not open to the public. The home which has been built at his birthplace site in North Fairfield, Vermont, is a replica of the original which was destroyed long ago.

A replica of the birthplace of President Chester A. Arthur at Fairfield, Vermont. The original was destroyed many years ago. (Vermont
Division for Historic Preservation)

22. and 24. Grover Cleveland

Grover Cleveland is the only President to have been elected twice without succeeding himself. Defeated for re-election by Benjamin Harrison in 1888, he in turn defeated President Harrison in 1892 and became President once again.

President Cleveland was born in 1837 in Caldwell, New Jersey, where his father was the minister of the First Presbyterian Church. Although he spent only his first three years in the comfortable house on Bloomfield Avenue, the furnishings and mementos in it today reflect his entire life. In the back bedroom is the wooden cradle in which he was rocked as a baby. In the living room is a rocking chair in which he rocked as the President. The desk he used while mayor of Buffalo, New York, is on display as well as many pictures and letters from friends and political acquaintances.

One unusual item of interest in this house is a box containing some wedding cake served to guests when President Cleveland married Frances Folsom on June 2, 1886. He was the only President to be married in the White House.

After his second term of office, President Cleveland and his family moved to a home in Princeton, New Jersey. They immediately began to remodel and add such a large wing to the back that it was later detached to form a separate home.

President Cleveland enjoyed his years of retirement. Students from Princeton University serenaded him on each birthday. When victorious football parades marched past his house, he always stepped out on his balcony to lead a cheer or two. He even helped a member of the faculty who needed a place to live by building a small cottage for him on his own estate. But it had one flaw—the basement soon filled with water. When the professor hesitantly mentioned it to his famous landlord, President Cleveland laughingly replied, "Well, my good fellow, what did you expect, champagne?"

23. Benjamin Harrison

Benjamin Harrison was a young lawyer and politician when Abraham Lincoln stopped in Indianapolis, Indiana, on his way to Washington and the Presidency. Benjamin remembered that Lincoln didn't look particularly happy and vowed to help his administration.

Sometime later, after President Lincoln's call for troops, Benjamin recruited soldiers for the Indiana 70th Volunteer Infantry Regiment. He served as its commander, and was discharged with the rank of brigadier general. It had been his duty as a Harrison, he later remarked, to serve his President and his country.

The Harrisons had been doing it for generations. His great-grandfather had signed the Declaration of Independence, his grandfather was the ninth President of the United States and his father had been a congressman. Now it was Benjamin's turn.

When Mr. Harrison returned to Indianapolis from the Civil War, he continued his successful law practice, and entered politics. In 1874, he built a home at 1230 North Delaware Street for his wife and two children. It had sixteen rooms, including two parlors of the same size, a library which was Mr. Harrison's favorite room and a third-floor ballroom. The solid, red brick house was surrounded by giant elms and oaks, and a picket fence.

The home of President Benjamin Harrison in Indianapolis was a center of the city's social life in the 1880s. The Harrisons were leading citizens of that city, and nothing proves it more than this big town house. (Arthur Jordan Foundation)

He was considered a "front-porch" campaigner because his political campaigns were conducted from home. But the massive front porch seen on the house today was not built until after Mr. Harrison won the election in 1888. However, while campaigning for the Presidency, he stood on the small front stoop outside the parlor window. There, he gave neighborly chats that attracted as many as 10,000 people in a single evening. When it was announced that he had won the election, the large crowd, which had gathered outside, tore down his picket fence and carried it away for souvenirs.

Although he did not win re-election in 1892, his house remained the focal point of political and social activity for many years. Mr. Harrison was a gifted speaker, and went on lecture tours around the country.

Once, while lecturing at Stanford University, he decided to attend the college baseball game, but entered the athletic field without buying a ticket. A few moments later, the manager of the Stanford team approached him and mentioned the oversight. The ex-President immediately apologized and bought a twenty-five cent ticket, then said to the manager, "What's your name?"

The student replied, "Herbert Hoover." (Hoover was to become our 31st President.)

25. William McKinley

When William McKinley married Ida Saxton in 1871, they moved into a white frame house on North Market Street in Canton, Ohio, which had been a wedding gift from her father. After Mr. McKinley was elected to Congress in 1876, they sold their home and spent the next years in Washington, D.C. and Columbus, Ohio. He was re-elected six times to Congress before serving two terms as governor of Ohio.

During the twenty years of Mr. McKinley's public life, he and his wife never owned another house. In 1896, they returned to Canton to live and found their old home was for rent. They moved in immediately.

When Mr. McKinley was nominated for the Presidency a few months later, his advisors planned a stay-at-home campaign. Soon the political world and sightseers came to their doorstep. As election neared, the white iron fence around the house, the grape arbor and Mrs. McKinley's rose bushes disappeared as souvenirs. The campaign led to Mr. McKinley's election and, four years later, he was re-elected.

The McKinleys spent the summer of 1901 at their home on North Market Street. The only formal duty the President had was at the opening of the Pan American Exposition in Buffalo, New York. Advised not to mingle with so many people at such close range, President McKinley said, "I have no enemies."

He had one. He was shot and died eight days later on September 6, 1901.

The North Market Street house was abandoned in the 1930s, and later torn down. A memorial library erected near Mr. McKinley's birthplace in Niles, Ohio, and a tomb in Canton are the only remaining structures associated with the 25th President.

26. Theodore Roosevelt

The sickly, frail twelve-year-old boy listened as his father talked to him in their home at 28 East 20th Street, in New York City. He had brains, his father said, but they were no good without a body. He must develop a body to match his brains.

From that time on, young Theodore worked hard to improve his physical health. He practiced lifting weights, and spent much time in the fresh air and sunshine, participating in rough and tumble sports. The young boy had set a pattern for his future. He would combine the outdoor life with the pursuit of knowledge.

Theodore Roosevelt was only twenty-six when he planned and built the house called "Sagamore Hill" on Oyster Bay, Long Island. Although his future would take him to jungles and battlefields, conference tables and meetings among nation's leaders around the world, he would always return to Sagamore Hill.

When Mr. Roosevelt brought his bride home in 1887, the former Edith Kermit Carow saw that the twenty-two room house was already crowded with prizes from his outdoor life. Soon the entire house overflowed with wild animal heads and pelts, and a trophy room was added in 1905.

The birthplace of Theodore Roosevelt in New York City. Although the Roosevelts owned this property when Theodore was born in 1858, the original house no longer exists. The present building is an exact duplicate, completed in 1923. On the third floor porch at the back of the house, young Theodore built his gymnasium where he worked hard to grow strong. (National Park Service)

Sagamore Hill, at Oyster Bay, Long Island, New York State. It was built in 1885, and Theodore Roosevelt lived there from that date until his death in 1919. During the years he was President, this home served as the summer White House. (National Park Service)

The trophy room at Sagamore Hill was added in 1905. It was designed to receive distinguished guests from all over the world, and
to show off the President's interest in wildlife and the outdoors.
(National Park Service)

How someone, like Theodore Rosoevelt, who became known as a conservationist could kill so many animals is difficult to explain. However, in the time in which he lived, the sport of big-game hunting was popular among men of his social class, and they had strict rules of good sportsmanship by which they hunted. Mr. Roosevelt also realized that wildlife needed protection in set-aside areas of the country if they were to survive. During his Presidency, he added 150,000,000 acres to our national forests, and expanded the number of national parks and monuments.

Colonel Roosevelt became a national hero after he led the Rough Riders in the Spanish-American War. In 1900, he was elected Vice-President, and after President McKinley's death, he became the President.

For seven years, Sagamore Hill was considered the summer White House as the nation followed the adventures of the six Roosevelt children and their ten cousins who lived nearby. Often the President stopped working on affairs of state to join in their outdoor games.

During his lifetime, the President's library served as his study and office. It was here that he wrote most of his 40 books and more than 3,000 newspaper and magazine articles. It was also in this room that he conducted the peace negotiations between Russia and Japan which won him the Nobel Peace Prize. Here, he was surrounded by statues, paintings, stuffed animals and other mementos of his busy life.

The library at Sagamore Hill. This room, together with the trophy room, contain most of President Theodore Roosevelt's personal belongings, books, rifles and trophies. (National Park Service)

27. William Howard Taft

Two months after William Howard Taft was born, his mother wrote to a relative. She said the baby "is perfectly healthy and hearty. He is very large for his age and grows fat every day."

As the boy grew up in the big, white brick house on Auburn Avenue in Cincinnati, Ohio, William continued to be large for his age. He and his four brothers spent most of their free time outside where they played in the family orchard and stables, "doing mischief generally," their mother reported.

The boys all swam, skated, and played baseball. Baseball was William's favorite game. Because of his size, he wasn't speedy on the base paths, but he could swing a bat and throw a ball with more strength than most boys his age. His interest in baseball, as well as in golf and swimming, continued into adulthood as he looked for some form of exercise that would help him lose some weight. It was President Taft who began the custom of throwing out the first ball, officially beginning a new baseball season.

After graduation from law school and marriage, he began his long career in public life. He never lived in the family home again, but in many other houses around the nation and the world. Soon he was appointed by governors and Presidents to positions of influence and importance. One appointment took him to the Philippines as governor of the newly won islands. His oversize bathtub was sent along. It was said that ten little Filipino boys could splash in it at the same time.

The boyhood home of President William Howard Taft at Cincinnati, Ohio. The picture was taken when Taft was 13 years old. He is standing behind the fence. (National Park Service)

He became Secretary of War in President Theodore Roosevelt's cabinet. When it seemed that the President would not run again, Mr. Taft's name began to be mentioned as a candidate.

One night when Mr. and Mrs. Taft were dining at the White House, President Roosevelt said, "I see a man weighing three hundred and fifty pounds. There is something hanging over his head. I cannot see what it is. At one time it looks like the presidency. Then again it looks like the chief justiceship." Mrs. Taft said, "Make it the presidency." Mr. Taft replied, "Make it the chief justiceship."

Both Mr. and Mrs. Taft's wishes came true. Some years after his one term, President Taft became Chief Justice of the Supreme Court, the only President in our history to serve in both high offices.

28. Woodrow Wilson

Thomas Woodrow Wilson (he dropped Thomas in college) spent less than a year in his birthplace at 24 North Coalter Street in Staunton, Virginia, but the house is furnished with possessions that he collected throughout his life. Some of them are a bookcase that he bought with the first money he earned, a desk, a chair and lamp he used while president of Princeton Unviersity, musical instruments that he and his wife played, and a 1919 Pierce Arrow car which he used while President of the United States.

In 1885, he married Ellen Lousie Axson with whom he had three daughters. She died in 1914, and the next year he married Edith Bolling Galt.

Nearing the end of President Wilson's second term, his wife Edith began to look for a house they might buy in which they could retire and live quietly. President Wilson's search for lasting international peace had won him the Nobel Peace Prize in 1919, but had lost him his health.

One day Mrs. Wilson saw a town house at 2340 S Street N.W. in Washington, D.C. She told her husband about it, but was completely surprised when he gave it to her on their fifth wedding anniversary. Taking her to the house, he followed a Scottish custom by presenting her with a piece of sod from the garden as well as the key to the front door.

The birthplace of Woodrow Wilson, in Staunton, Virginia, was built in 1846, in a style known as Greek Revival. The back portico shown in this photo looks down on a lovely Victorian garden. (Virginia State Travel Service)

The Washington, D.C. home of President Wilson was his retirement home, and is the place where he died after three years of illness. He is the only President buried in the city of Washington, D.C. (Photo by Marler)

The library of President Wilson's Washington, D.C. home. Wilson's portrait hangs above the fireplace. He lived in quiet retirement here, trying to recover his health. It was a losing battle. (Photo by Marler)

They moved in on the day they left the White House, after first putting in an elevator and building shelves for the ex-President's 8,000 books. Mr. Wilson began to spend much of his time in the library which was lined from floor to ceiling with the books he had used while a professor and president of Princeton University. His favorite chair is still pulled up by the fireplace. A small table in the library is set with cards he used while playing his favorite baseball card game. These are actual playing cards with specific instructions on them for what each player is to do. The person who is drawing the card is considered at bat and follows instructions on the card he draws, such as "strike out," "base hit," etc.

Every table and mantel throughout the house contains clocks, photographs, statues and other gifts sent to the President by the public and world leaders. Because he could walk only with the aid of a cane during his last years, he was sent many canes. They, too, are still in the house.

Only on special occasions did President Wilson leave his house. Sometimes he went for rides around the city and country, and once in a while, he went to the movies and the theater.

Once a year, he would go to a front window of his home and wave to the many people gathered there who came to salute him on Armistice Day. They came again on the gray February day he died in 1924.

29. Warren G. Harding

Warren Harding was a hard working newspaper editor in Marion, Ohio, when he met Florence deWolfe. Soon they wanted to marry, but her parents objected because they felt Warren wasn't good enough for their daughter. Despite her parents' objections, the young couple went ahead with their plans and began to build their dream home.

When it was finished at 380 Mount Vernon Avenue, they were married in its large front hallway in July, 1891. Although the new Mrs. Harding's father didn't speak to her for years after her marriage, he was impressed by the large house with its tiled floor on the porch, gas grates which provided heat for the rooms, and a stained glass window.

Warren Harding served Ohio as state senator, lieutenant governor and U.S. senator. In 1920, he was nominated for the Presidency and conducted his campaign from his house, as had become the custom of those times.

He made many front-porch speeches, and had his lawn replaced by gravel to accommodate the crowds. After his speeches, he visited with many of the politicians and campaigners, shaking hands with as many as he could reach. "It's the most pleasant thing I do," he once said.

When he was elected President, the Hardings put their furniture and possessions in storage. First, however, they made a

Home of President Warren G. Harding, at Marion, Ohio. The Harding house was a political center. Mrs. Harding helped her husband to build his newspaper, the Marion *Star,* into a prosperous enterprise, and to use it to make friends and start the campaign that would end with Harding's election as President. (Photo by Dale E. Hughes, Inc.)

chart to show where each piece belonged. After Mr. Harding's death in office, his widow never returned to live in the house she had helped to plan and build. She died a year later, leaving over 2,000 items of furnishings and mementos to an association which owns the house today. When the house was restored, all the possessions were put back in their original places, using the chart the Hardings had made.

30. Calvin Coolidge

"It seemed a simple and natural thing to do at the time." Those are the words used by Calvin Coolidge in his autobiography to describe the most important moment of his life. He was speaking of 2:47 A.M. on August 3, 1923 when he was sworn in as President of the United States by his father in the sitting room of his boyhood home in Plymouth Notch, Vermont.

The Coolidge home is one of the most authentic and completely furnished farmhouses of the period. Since 1876, when Calvin Coolidge's father bought it, the house remained in the family until 1957 when it was given to the state of Vermont. It wasn't difficult for historians to restore the house to the way it looked on the morning of August 3, 1923.

The heart of the house was always the kitchen, used not only for cooking and eating, but for entertaining guests. Standing outside the back door, young Calvin often had to overcome his natural shyness in order to go inside when his parents had company.

Today, the kitchen table is set just as it always was with plates and cups placed upside down, ready for the next meal. Standing by the sink is the woodbox which Calvin always kept filled. The big, black stove in the center of the room is polished and shining as if from a recent scrubbing.

Homestead of President Calvin Coolidge, at Plymouth Notch, Vermont. It was in this home (which belonged to his father at the time) that Vice-President Calvin Coolidge retired for the night on August 2, 1923. He was awakened at 2 a.m. and told that President Harding had died. Coolidge got up, went downstairs to the parlor and had his father swear him in as the 30th President of the United States. (Vermont Division for Historic Preservation)

Young Calvin left this house to go to school and enter politics, but he always returned for a summer holiday. He had been vacationing from his duties as Vice-President when the telegram came about President Harding's death. Reporters arrived also, and one of them reminded Mr. Coolidge that the country now had no President. It was then that he asked his father if he was still a notary public. (A notary public is a person authorized by law to administer oaths in addition to other duties.) The older man said yes and the Vice-President replied, "I want you to administer the oath."

President Calvin Coolidge taking the oath of office in the Parlor at the family homestead. His mother's Bible was used in the ceremony. (Library of Congress)

After looking up the correct words to use, Mr. Coolidge, his father, his wife, Grace, and several others stepped into the sitting room. There by the light of a kerosene lamp, Mr. Coolidge repeated the words read by his father which made him the President of the United States.

After that short and simple ceremony, the new President went back to bed and slept soundly the rest of the night.

31. Herbert Hoover

Herbert Hoover was born in West Branch, Iowa, on August 10, 1874 in a two-room cottage near the blacksmith shop owned by his father. Although he spent only the first ten years of his life in West Branch, President Hoover never forgot the lessons about honesty, loyalty, generosity and hard work that his Quaker parents taught him.

Birthplace of President Herbert Hoover, at West Branch, Iowa. This two-room cottage has been furnished with many of the original pieces which belonged to Mr. Hoover's parents, who built the home about 1870. (National Park Service)

After his parents died he was sent to live with relatives. He studied engineering at Stanford University in California, and after graduation became a mining engineer and traveled around the world many times. He became very successful and well known, and mining companies paid him well.

World War I began in 1914, and he was asked to organize a relief committee to help hungry people in Europe. Then President Wilson invited him to become food administrator for the United States after it entered the war in 1917. Mr. Hoover immediately asked American families to stop wasting food. The slogan "Save a loaf (of bread) a week, help win the war" became popular. He also gained the help of American farmers by promising fair prices for the food they grew. As a result, Mr. Hoover kept American armies fed, and he built up supplies of food in Europe that saved many people from starvation.

When the war ended, he was offered a job that would have paid him more than half a million dollars a year. Instead, he turned it down to become Secretary of Commerce for much less. Mr. Hoover had told friends earlier, "I know how to make money, now I want to be of service." When he was elected to the Presidency in 1928, he banked his salary and later donated it all to charity. Throughout his career in government, he never took a penny in salary and even paid his own expenses! His wife explained this, saying, "He had deeply ingrained in him the Quaker feeling that nothing matters if you are right with God."

After he was defeated for re-election in 1932, ex-President Hoover continued to work for his country. In 1946, President Harry Truman asked him to study food supplies and advise what could be done to avoid starvation around the world. As

Bedroom of President Hoover's birthplace. At left is an old sewing ➤ machine, and on top of the bureau is a kerosene lamp. Both were necessary items in most homes of the late nineteenth century, especially the small farmsteads of the Mid-West. (National Park Service)

a result of World War II, food supplies were dangerously low nearly everywhere. President Truman said, "He did a job for me that nobody else in the world could have done. He kept millions of people from starving to death after the second World War just as he did after the first World War. What more can a man do?"

In 1962, President Hoover returned to West Branch on his 88th birthday to dedicate the library that had been built to hold his collection of papers, books, and memories. (Presidential libraries have been built for most modern presidents beginning with Hoover. Nixon, Ford and Carter libraries have not yet been started.)

The walk from the library crosses the Wapsinonoc Creek where as a child the President caught fish and gathered stones so long ago. It leads to the cottage, which is furnished once again in the same homespun style as when Mr. Hoover lived

there. The walnut cradle his father made for him and his brother and sister stands in the bedroom near the sewing machine his mother used to make their clothes. The table in the parlor is near the back door, just a step from the summer kitchen.

President Hoover's life took him to all parts of the world and touched millions of people during his ninety years. But he never forgot the Quaker lessons he learned in the simple two-room cottage at West Branch, Iowa.

32. Franklin Delano Roosevelt

Once, when Franklin D. Roosevelt was a young boy, his mother found him reading the dictionary in bed. When asked why, he told her it was because there were "so many words he didn't know."

That bed is still in his bedroom at the family home in Hyde Park, New York. Franklin Roosevelt was born there, educated at home until he was fourteen, then went to Groton School, Harvard University and Columbia Law School before beginning his political career. But Hyde Park was always home, even though he lived in another one, the White House, for twelve years.

Franklin was a collector all his life. He collected stamps, birds, ship models and naval prints, all of which can be seen at his home or in the Presidential library next door.

When he and his mother decided to enlarge and remodel the house, Franklin enthusiastically made a collection of wooden models, showing the changes. Additions, made of stucco and brick, were built on the north and south ends of the original farmhouse. A portico was added to the front and a terrace to the back.

Today, the visitor can see the thirty-five room house as it was finished in 1916. From the front portico, Franklin announced in 1920 that he would run for Vice-President.

Back in 1905, he had married Anna Eleanor Roosevelt, a distant cousin of his and the niece of Theodore Roosevelt.

The living room of the 30-room mansion at Hyde Park, home of Franklin Delano Roosevelt. The "fireside chats" of Depression and World War II fame were broadcast by radio from this room, which, at the time, also served as the main library. Mr. Roosevelt was born here and lived here most of his life. It is also where both he and his wife Eleanor are buried. (National Park Service)

They had four sons and a daughter. In August of 1921 at Campobello Island, their summer home at the time, Mr. Roosevelt was stricken with poliomyelitis. He was paralyzed from the waist down, but through hard work he recovered partial use of his legs. Although crippled to the end of his life, it did not stop him from having an active public career.

He was Assistant Secretary of the Navy, Governor of New York and President of the United States.

Hyde Park became known as the summer White House after Mr. Roosevelt's election to the Presidency in 1932. Winston Churchill, prime minister of England, and Mr. Roosevelt often met there during World War II. On June 20, 1942, they signed an agreement in his office at home, beginning the research program that created the atomic bomb.

Throughout his presidential years, President Roosevelt broadcast many of his "fireside chats" over the radio from the large library-living room. These were talks the President gave to the nation as he sat by his fireside.

The Roosevelts loved to entertain at Hyde Park. In the summer of 1939, the King and Queen of England came to visit. Instead of having a grand party indoors, President and Mrs. Roosevelt gave a picnic for their visitors, serving them hot dogs and strawberry shortcake!

On November 6, 1944, President Roosevelt broadcast his last campaign speech from his office at home. He was elected to a fourth term, but did not live to complete it. He died on April 12, 1945 and is buried at Hyde Park, his home from his first day to his last.

33. Harry S Truman

In his autobiography, *Mr. Citizen*, Harry S Truman said, "In all the years since I left the White House, I have wondered why so many people come from so far away and take so much trouble to look at the house where I live."

He was referring to his home in Independence, Missouri, but he could also have been talking about his birthplace in Lamar, Missouri. This house is open to visitors; the one in Independence is still occupied by the family and is not open to the public.

The small, six-room house in Lamar was purchased from its owners and given to the state by the United Auto Workers in 1957. Then began a time of restoring it to look as it did when the house had no electricity, running water, attic, clothes closets or bathrooms. The rooms were very small. The bedroom in which Harry was born measures less than seven by eleven feet, about twice the size of his Presidential desk.

The Trumans left this house when Harry was only a baby. He began school in Independence, later farmed, and worked in Kansas City. After service in World War I, he returned to Independence and married Bess Wallace, his childhood sweetheart. They moved into the Wallace home at 219 North Delaware Street, and it became their permanent home. Throughout his long years in the Senate, then as Vice-President and President, the Trumans returned as often as they could to the only home they ever owned.

Mr. Truman won election to the Vice-Presidency in 1944, and came to the Presidency following Mr. Roosevelt's death on April 12, 1945. It was a difficult time for the nation and the world. President Truman decided to use the atomic bomb against Japan to end World War II. He helped to slow the spread of communism through military agreements (NATO) with other countries, and began an airlift of supplies to the people of West Berlin when the Soviet Union blockaded the divided city. President Truman also backed the program of Secretary of State George C. Marshall to help countries of Europe rebuild after the war (the Marshall Plan).

The United Nations had just been organized when Mr. Truman came to office, and it looked to the United States for leadership. The President provided it by proposing world control of atomic energy and later, defending South Korea from invasion by North Korea with United States and United Nations troops working together.

Mr. Truman was re-elected in 1948, but decided not to seek another term in 1952. The Trumans came home to the house on North Delaware Street once again, this time to stay.

34. Dwight D. Eisenhower

When Dwight Eisenhower was a teenager, he became ill with blood poisoning in a badly infected leg. For awhile the doctor thought his leg might have to be amputated, but Dwight said no. For days, he lay in his big oak bed and fought the poison that ran through his body. Many weeks later, Dwight recovered and returned to school. Later, he went on to West Point and the future—to become one of the world's best known leaders. But he never forgot his first major battle, fought in the bedroom of his Abilene, Kansas home.

His parents bought the house and land when Dwight was eight, and they found it was an ideal place to raise their six sons. Along with the nearly three acres of land on which to raise food, there were wide open fields for the boys to explore. For excitement, the Parker merry-go-round factory and winter carnival grounds were just a short distance away.

Mr. and Mrs. Eisenhower continued to live in the small house after their sons were grown. Throughout the years, they returned on visits to bring gifts and tell of their work in business, law, and the Army which took them to exciting parts of the world.

The bedroom of President Dwight D. Eisenhower's boyhood home in Abilene, Kansas. There is one thing in this room that we never saw in the homes of the early presidents—electric lights. (General Services Administration)

Although Dwight Eisenhower never again lived in Abilene after he left for West Point in 1911, the house and its furnishings reflect much of his life. When the six Eisenhower brothers deeded the home to the government, they asked that it remain exactly as it was when the family lived there.

The furnishings are plain and inexpensive throughout the white frame house. The piano in the living room was Mrs.

The front parlor of President Eisenhower's boyhood home. Here, for the first time, we see a radio as a regular piece of furniture. It is sitting in the corner with a clock on top of it. Those old-fashioned radios were nearly always large, important pieces of furniture. (General Services Administration)

Eisenhower's pride and joy, and she often played for relaxation at the end of the day. She taught all her sons, but only two, Milton and Arthur, played.

In 1932, Dwight gave his mother a set of six plates honoring the two hundredth anniversary of George Washington's birth. The plates are displayed on the buffet in the dining room directly behind the silver coffee service the boys gave their parents on their fiftieth wedding anniversary. Another of their gifts is the radio on the walnut table in the living room. The photograph of Mrs. Eisenhower above the bookcase in the hall was taken at the time General Eisenhower received his promotion to four-star rank in February, 1943.

After World War II ended, the General and his wife, Mamie, began to look for a home they could live in permanently. They bought a farm near Gettysburg, Pennsylvania, in 1950 and hoped to move in the following year. However, the General was nominated for the Presidency in 1952 and was re-elected in 1956. After his years of service to the country ended in 1960, the Eisenhowers retired to the Pennsylvania farm, the only land they ever owned.

The 15-room house, on 189 acres, is at the edge of the Gettysburg National Battlefield. The General's worn, blue, felt-covered rocking chair is on the back porch where he liked to entertain visitors or paint portraits. Nearby is Mamie Eisenhower's card table, where she played solitaire or watched television soap operas.

The Eisenhowers donated the farm and grounds to the government in 1967. It was to become a national historic site after their deaths. The General died in 1969, his wife ten years later. The site was opened to the public on June 15, 1980.

35. John F. Kennedy

When you visit John F. Kennedy's birthplace at 83 Beals Street in Brookline, Massachusetts, his mother, Mrs. Rose Kennedy, will guide you through via a tape recorded tour. The house was sold by the Kennedys in 1921, purchased back by them in 1966 and given to the government. Since then, Mrs. Kennedy has supervised the restoration of the house to the way it looked when young John was growing up.

The piano in the living room was given to the Kennedys as a wedding present. The gateleg table and the vases on the mantle stand in the same place as they did over sixty years ago. Young John and his sisters and older brother played on the oriental rug.

Upstairs, the master bedroom is arranged exactly as it was on that sunny May day in 1917 when John was born. All of the furnishings are in place from the beds and dresser to the hair brushes and bud vases. Wedding announcements, photographs and other reminders of family life hang on the walls to tell a continuing story about the Kennedy family.

The bassinet in the nursery was used for all the children. So were the christening gown, bonnet and cape.

When John was four, the family moved to a larger house on Naples Road. It is within easy walking distance of the Beals Street house and is part of the tour designed to show visitors the neighborhood where the thirty-fifth President lived.

The birthplace of President John F. Kennedy, at 83 Beals Street, Brookline, Massachusetts, a suburb of Boston. This is a typical middle-income urban home of the early twentieth century. But the Kennedy family moved often, and always to wealthier neighborhoods, as Mr. Kennedy became a successful investment banker and financier. (National Park Service)

Mr. Kennedy received most of his early education at private schools, and graduated from Harvard University with honors in political science. In 1941, he became an ensign in the U.S. Navy and saw action in the Pacific during World War II. He was elected to Congress, first as a representative and then as a senator in 1952. The following year he married Jacqueline Bouvier.

When John F. Kennedy became President in 1961, he began the Peace Corps to help other nations. He also took the responsibility for the Bay of Pigs invasion of Cuba, an attempt by a group of Cubans to overthrow Fidel Castro, the dictator of Cuba. When the communists built a wall to isolate West Berlin, Kennedy delivered his famous "I am a Berliner" speech at the wall, in support of West German democracy. He began a number of reforms and defended minority rights in the United States, but did not live to see his work finished. He was shot and killed on November 22, 1963, the fourth American President to be assassinated.

36. Lyndon B. Johnson

After the death of John F. Kennedy, Lyndon Johnson became President. His many years as a senator helped him in his relationship with Congress. Together, they passed many laws, including the Civil Rights Act of 1964, which established fair employment practices for everyone, regardless of color. Johnson was re-elected in 1964, but soon he began to be criticized for some of his actions, especially sending more and more troops to fight in Vietnam. Debate over this undeclared war divided the country, and there were many riots and demonstrations. In March of 1968, Johnson announced that he would not be a candidate for re-election, and retired with Mrs. Johnson to the LBJ Ranch in Texas. He died there in 1973.

Mrs. Johnson has written these thoughts about the LBJ Ranch especially for this book.

"The original part of what is now the LBJ Ranch house was built of local fieldstone in 1892 by a German family named Meyer and consisted of one large room, a shed room out back and a loft-bedroom for the children. The old fireplace in the original structure, now the living room, is as it was in those early days, with the crane used for cooking still there.

"Lyndon's aunt and uncle, Mr. and Mrs. Clarence Martin, purchased the house in 1912 when Lyndon was four years old. That fireplace was the center of many family gatherings during Lyndon's childhood. He and his brothers and sisters and cousins would stand by the fireside, and in the custom of the times, recite poetry and join in singing songs. No doubt it's where he made his first speech!

"Lyndon and I bought the ranch from the Martins in 1951. During the following years, Lyndon and I enlarged the bedroom and the dining room and added several bathrooms and dressing rooms, and most importantly, an office wing.

"The house is filled with family treasures, a few valuable and nearly all very sentimental. There are gifts from friends and my own favorite piece of furniture, a table made from a slab of oak from Sherwood Forest. (The tree fell in a storm after standing since the days of Robin Hood some 1400 years ago.)

The Lyndon B. Johnson Ranch, at Stonewall, Texas. This Texas ranch house is not very different from the plantation type southern homestead, except that cattle were often the mainstay of the ranch, as this picture shows. President Johnson was born near here, but his birthplace is little more than a shack. (National Park Service)

"Our living room has been the scene of many happy times. I think of the games of dominos which Lyndon relished, an evening spent entertaining the President of Mexico with all of us singing to guitar music, and everyone of our family Christmases except for 1967 and 68 which were spent at the White House. Lyndon's favorite chair, a beige-corduroy recliner given him by his staff, was always by the telephone.

"Rooms which will one day be open to the public include Lyndon's office (presently the West Room where I entertain), and the Yellow Room which is now my favorite place to play cards with friends and grandchildren.

"Lyndon loved this house and surrounding countryside from the days of his earliest childhood."

The living room of the LBJ ranch. Among the interesting things in this room are the great open fireplace with the hanging iron pot that was used for cooking, and the fine collection of Indian arrowheads on the wall at left. (National Park Service)

37. Richard Nixon

Frank Nixon moved from Ohio in 1907 and worked at a variety of jobs before settling down in the small community of Yorba Linda, California, five years later. There, he built a small framehouse in which his son, Richard Milhous, was born on January 9, 1913.

Mr. and Mrs. Nixon were active in the civic and religious life of their community, and helped found the local Quakers, or Friends, Church where their children attended Sunday School. Richard went to public school in town and had completed third grade before his father's citrus farm became unprofitable. Then the family moved to nearby Whittier.

After the Nixons left, their house was bought and sold to a number of people. In the late '40s, the Yorba Linda School District bought the property. Several times the house faced destruction due to building programs considered by the school. Each time, however, the house was saved, and at last, the citizens of Yorba Linda had it designated as an historic site.

Several years ago, the property was bought by the Nixon Birthplace Foundation which plans to open the house to the public at a future time. When it is open, visitors will see the small white house standing in a grove of trees at the top of a knoll. At the entrance to the property is a marker made of rocks from all the states in the Union. In the house, there will be more than two thousand items collected by the Foundation over the years, including the piano and violin President Nixon practiced on as a child.

The piano moved with Mr. and Mrs. Nixon to the East when their son became Vice-President in 1952. When they later retired to Florida, the piano was given to friends for safekeeping. Many years later, the Foundation located the piano, and it made another cross-country journey to the house in Yorba Linda it left long ago.

President Nixon returns occasionally to his birthplace to take pictures and reminisce with friends. His recollections include stories of his political life which began when he became a representative in the U.S. Congress in 1946. From the House, he went to the Senate until his election as Vice-President in 1952. He lost the Presidential election in 1960, but won in 1968 and again in 1972.

Mr. Nixon's White House years saw many changes in this country's relationships with other countries. He brought an end to American participation in the Vietnam War, and arranged for the release of American prisoners. In 1972, he visited the People's Republic of China, opening the way to contact between the two nations after many years. Later that same year, and again in 1974, Mr. Nixon visited the Soviet Union to sign treaties to limit the manufacture and stocking of nuclear weapons.

In his second term of office, a series of suspicious activities by members of a re-election committee led to an investigation. Soon it was known as the Watergate affair because the activity had begun in a hotel called Watergate. Some of Mr. Nixon's cabinet members and aides were convicted of acting illegally and were sent to prison. Suspicion was also thrown on Mr. Nixon himself. A Congressional committee found reasons for possibly impeaching the President. But before impeachment started, Mr. Nixon resigned on August 9, 1974, the first President to do so.

President Gerald R. Ford is shown here when he was a member of ➤ the University of Michigan football team. Jerry was his team's most valuable player in his senior year. (University of Michigan Information Service)

38. Gerald R. Ford

Gerald Ford is a man who is used to winning. He has won many titles, positions and awards during his lifetime, except the most important one of all—the President of the United States. To that position, he was appointed.

At South High in Grand Rapids, Michigan, young Jerry starred as center on the football team and won the honor of becoming team captain. In 1934, he was elected the most valuable player of the University of Michigan's football team.

When he graduated, he could have gone on to play professional football. Instead, he went to law school, then became an officer in the U.S. Navy during World War II. He returned to Grand Rapids when the war ended, and ran for the House of Representatives. After winning the election in 1948, he won it twelve more times. He served twenty-five years in the House before he was appointed Vice-President in 1973, succeeding Spiro Agnew, who had resigned.

Following President Nixon's resignation in 1974, Gerald Ford became the first President who had never campaigned in a nationwide election. After he assumed the office, President Ford's job became one of restoring trust in the government since the Watergate affair had shaken public confidence.

Gerald Ford was born Leslie Lynch King, Jr. on July 14, 1913. Two years later, his parents were divorced, and the following year his mother married Gerald R. Ford. He adopted Leslie and gave the boy his name.

When Jerry Ford was eight years old, he and his family moved into a house on Union Street in Grand Rapids. To keep the house clean and shining, he and his three brothers were given chores to do. Between six and six-thirty every winter morning, Jerry had to remove the ashes from the furnace and put in the day's supply of coal. During the summer, he mowed the lawn and helped clean the garage. Each member of the family made his own bed and took his turn in the kitchen.

But the four boys had fun, too. At the rear of the property there was an old two-story garage. The boys and their friends enjoyed playing cards on the second floor, sure that their parents didn't know. But their parents did find out, and they were punished. It was also an end to the card games.

The house on Union Street has recently been purchased by the city of Grand Rapids. It has not yet been restored nor is it open to the public. A Presidential library is planned at Ann Arbor, Michigan, and a Ford Museum will open in Grand Rapids in 1981.

39. Jimmy Carter

Jimmy Carter was born in Plains, Georgia, but moved with his family to a nearby smaller community of Archery when he was four. There, Jimmy's father farmed cotton, peanuts and other crops, and opened a small store next to the house.

In winter, the house was heated by fireplaces and the wood stove in the kitchen. Jimmy's bedroom had no heat except for hot bricks and a fluffy down comforter which helped warm his cold bed.

In summer, the house was cooled by a low overhanging porch that wrapped around three sides of the frame house. The summers were long and hot in Georgia, lasting from mid-April until the end of September. During that time, Jimmy seldom wore shoes.

For many years, there was no electricity in the house. In the evenings, Jimmy and his family read by the light of kerosene lamps, and listened to a battery-operated radio. He particularly enjoyed listening to political conventions and speeches and the music of Glenn Miller, a popular orchestra leader in the '30s.

Jimmy's father believed hard work and thrift were necessary to become successful, and taught his son the value of both. During the depression years of the 1930s, Mr. Carter and his employees worked hard. They harvested crops which kept food on their tables and some money in their pockets when many people in the country were doing without either.

Jimmy had many jobs which occupied him as he grew up. He "toted" water for the farm hands, filled seed planters and fertilizer machines and ran errands. Finally the day came when he could plow with no one helping, but the mule.

However, life on the farm was not all work. There were long summer days when Jimmy and his friends could go fishing and swimming in nearby rivers and creeks. Sometimes his sisters, Gloria and Ruth, and his brother, Billy, went along, too. And there were other days when he went to Plains to sell bags of peanuts that were grown on the farm. That was fun, too, and he was earning his own money as well.

Jimmy saved his peanut money and by the time he was nine, he had enough to buy some bales of cotton. His father stored them until the price had gone high enough so that Jimmy could make a profit. With the money, Jimmy bought four houses in Plains which he rented out for a total of $16.50 a month. He was a homeowner at thirteen.

Jimmy went to the U.S. Naval Academy at Annapolis and pursued a naval career until 1953, when his father died. Then he returned to Plains with his own young family to run the Carter peanut business.

For a few years, Mr. Carter, Rosalynn and the children lived in an old farmhouse on the edge of town. Then, in 1962, they built a one-story, ten room brick house on Woodland Drive. It was from this home that Mr. Carter began his political career which took him first to the Georgia legislature, and then to the governor's mansion. In 1975, he decided to run for the Presidency. Even though he was not known to many people, Mr. Carter worked hard campaigning across the nation. Soon people knew him and his platform, and he was elected in 1976.

President and Mrs. Carter's home in Plains is still used by them and their family, so it is not open to tourists. Other homes in which Mr. Carter lived are noted by signs, but at the present none are open to the public.

How To Get There

All of the following sites are open to the public, except where indicated. Although dates and hours of availability are listed, these are sometimes subject to change. Therefore, it is suggested that you inquire about visiting hours before you go. In some cases, admission is charged.

CALIFORNIA

Richard M. Nixon
Birthplace home is located at 18061 Yorba Linda Boulevard, Yorba Linda. Administered by the Nixon Birthplace Foundation. Not yet open to the public.

DISTRICT OF COLUMBIA

Woodrow Wilson
Wilson retirement home is located at 2340 S Street, N.W. Washington, D.C. Administered by the National Trust for Historic Preservation. Open daily Monday through Friday from 10 A.M. to 2 P.M. and Saturdays, Sundays, and holidays from noon to 4 P.M. Closed on Thanksgiving, Christmas and New Year's Day.

ILLINOIS

Ulysses S. Grant

Grant Home is located at 511 Bouthillier Street, Galena. Administered by State of Illinois, Department of Conservation. Open daily from 9 A.M. to 5 P.M. Closed on Thanksgiving, Christmas and New Year's Day.

Abraham Lincoln

Lincoln home is located at 526 South Seventh Street, Springfield. Administered by the National Park Service. Open daily from 8 A.M. to 5 P.M. Closed on Christmas and New Year's Day.

INDIANA

Benjamin Harrison

Harrison Home is located at 1230 North Delaware Street, Indianapolis. Owned by the Arthur Jordan Foundation and preserved by the President Benjamin Harrison Foundation. Open weekdays from 10 A.M. to 4 P.M., Sundays from 12:30 P.M. to 4 P.M.

William Henry Harrison

Grouseland is located at 3 West Scott Street, Vincennes. Owned and maintained by the Francis Vigo Chapter, Daughters of the American Revolution. Open daily 9 A.M. to 5 P.M. except Thanksgiving, Christmas and New Year's Day.

Abraham Lincoln

Boyhood National Memorial is located on Indiana Highway 345, four miles south of Dale. Administered by National Park Service.

IOWA

Herbert Hoover

Hoover Birthplace is located on Downey Street, West Branch.

Administered by National Park Service. Open daily from 8 A.M. to 5 P.M. Closed on Thanksgiving, Christmas and New Year's Day.

KANSAS

Dwight D. Eisenhower
Eisenhower Center is located on Southeast Fourth Street, Abilene. Maintained by the General Service Administration. Open daily from 9 A.M. to 5 P.M. Closed on Thanksgiving, Christmas and New Year's Day.

KENTUCKY

Abraham Lincoln
Lincoln Birthplace historic site is located just off U.S. Highway 31E, three miles south of Hodgenville. Administered by the National Park Service.

Zachary Taylor
Springfield is located at 5608 Apache Road, Louisville. Privately owned, it is not open to the public.

MASSACHUSETTS

John Adams and John Quincy Adams
Adams Birthplace is located at 141 Franklin Street, Quincy. Administered by the National Park Service. Open seven days a week 9 A.M. to 5 P.M. from April 19 to October 15. Outdoor interpretation only.

Adams Historical Site is located at 135 Adams Street, Quincy. Administered by the National Park Service. Open daily from April 19 to November 10, 9 A.M. to 5 P.M.

John F. Kennedy
Kennedy Birthplace is located at 83 Beals Street, Brookline. Ad-

ministered by the National Park Service. Open daily from 9 A.M. to 4:30 P.M. Closed Thanksgiving, Christmas and New Year's Day.

MISSOURI

Harry S. Truman

Truman Birthplace is located in Lamar. Maintained by the Division of Parks and Recreation, State of Missouri. Open daily from 10 A.M. to 4 P.M. Sundays from noon to 5 P.M. Closed on New Year's Day, Easter, Thanksgiving and Christmas Day.

Truman Historic District is on North Delaware Street and environs, Independence. Includes area where President lived, went to school and worked. Walking tours only.

NEW HAMPSHIRE

Franklin Pierce

Pierce Homestead is located three miles west of Hillsboro, New Hampshire. Administered by State of New Hampshire, Division of Parks. Open daily from Memorial Day to mid-October.

NEW JERSEY

Grover Cleveland

Cleveland Birthplace is located at 207 Bloomfield Avenue, Caldwell. Administered by the State of New Jersey, Department of Environmental Protection. Open Wednesday through Saturday, 9 A.M. to 6 P.M., Sundays 1 P.M. to 6 P.M.

Westland is located at 15 Hodge Road, Princeton. A National Historic Landmark, but privately owned and not open to the public.

NEW YORK

Chester A. Arthur

Arthur residence is located at 123 Lexington Avenue, New York

City. Privately owned, it is not open to the public.

Millard Fillmore
Fillmore home is located at 24 Shearer Avenue, East Aurora. Privately owned, it is not open to the public.

Franklin D. Roosevelt
Hyde Park is located on Albany Post Road, Hyde Park. Maintained by National Park Service. Open daily from 9 A.M. to 5 P.M. Closed Christmas and New Year's Day.

Theodore Roosevelt
Sagamore Hill is located on Cove Neck Road, Oyster Bay, New York. Administered by the National Park Service. Open daily 9:30 A.M. to 6 P.M. Closed Thanksgiving, Christmas and New Year's Day.

Birthplace is located at 28 East 20th Street, New York City. Administered by the National Park Service. Open seven days a week 9 A.M. to 5 P.M. Closed on Mondays and Tuesdays after Labor Day.

Martin Van Buren
Lindenwald is located on Highway 9 H, Columbia County, Kinderhook, New York. Administered by National Park Service. Limited portions of estate now open to visitors until completion in 1982.

OHIO

James A. Garfield
Lawnfield is located at 8095 Mentor Avenue in Mentor. Administered by the Lake County Historical Society. Open mid-April to mid-November Tuesdays through Saturdays, 9 A.M. to 5 P.M. Sundays and holidays 1 P.M. to 5 P.M.

Warren G. Harding

The Harding home is located at 380 Mt. Vernon Avenue, Marion. Maintained by the Harding Memorial Association. Open Wednesdays through Saturdays, 9:30 A.M. to 5 P.M. Sundays from 1 to 5 P.M. Closed Mondays and Tuesdays.

Rutherford B. Hayes

Spiegel Grove is located at 1337 Hayes Avenue, Fremont. Administered by the Hayes Foundation and Ohio Historical Society. Open Wednesdays through Saturdays 9 A.M. to 5 P.M., Sundays through Tuesdays 2 P.M. to 5 P.M. Closed Thanksgiving, Christmas and New Year's Day.

William McKinley

McKinley Memorial Library is located at 40 North Main Street, Niles. Open daily. Closed Thanksgiving, Christmas and New Year's Day.

William Howard Taft

The Taft home is located at 2038 Auburn Avenue, Cincinnati. Administered by the National Park Service. Open daily from 8 A.M. to 4:30 P.M. from Memorial Day to Labor Day. After Labor Day, open from 8 A.M. to 4:30 P.M. Monday through Friday. Closed weekends.

PENNSYLVANIA

James Buchanan

Wheatland is located at 1120 Marietta Avenue, Lancaster. Maintained by the James Buchanan Foundation for the Preservation of Wheatland and the Junior League of Lancaster. Open daily including Sunday from 10:00 A.M. to 5:00 P.M. from April 1st to December 1st.

Dwight D. Eisenhower

Eisenhower farm is located adjacent to the southwest boundary of Gettysburg National Military Park, Gettysburg. Administered by the National Park Service. From June through Labor Day, the house will be open daily from 9 A.M. to 4:30 P.M., the historic site grounds until 6:00 P.M. The tourist center, from which shuttle buses leave, is open from 8:00 A.M. to 5:00 P.M.

TENNESSEE

Andrew Jackson

The Hermitage is located on Old Hickory Boulevard, twelve miles northeast of Nashville. Administered by the Ladies' Hermitage Association. Open from June 1 through Labor Day from 8 A.M. to 6 P.M. Open the rest of the year from 9 A.M. to 5 P.M. Closed on Christmas Day.

Andrew Johnson

Johnson Homestead is on Main Street (U.S. Highway 411), Greeneville. Maintained by the National Park Service. Open daily from 9 A.M. to 5 P.M. Closed on Christmas Day.

James K. Polk

The Polk home is located at 301 West Seventh Street, Columbia. Maintained by the James K. Polk Association and Auxiliary. Open daily Monday through Saturday from 9 A.M. to 5 P.M. Half days on Sunday. Closed on Christmas Day.

TEXAS

Lyndon B. Johnson

Boyhood home is located in Johnson City, Texas. Administered by the National Park Service. Open 9 A.M. to 6 P.M. every day but Christmas.

Birthplace is located between Johnson City and Stonewall, Texas. LBJ Ranch is located near Stonewall, Texas, a mile west of the birthplace. Ranchhouse is not open to the public, but visitors may tour and view exteriors of buildings. Birthplace is included in Ranch bus tour which is available from 10 A.M. to 5:30 P.M. every day but Christmas. Administered by the National Park Service.

Dwight D. Eisenhower
Birthplace is located at 208 East Day Street, Denison. Open from 8 A.M. to 5 P.M. seven days a week, year round.

VERMONT

Chester A. Arthur
Arthur Birthplace is located in North Fairfield. Administered by Vermont Division of Historic Preservation. Open June through mid-October, Wednesday through Sunday from 9 A.M. to 5 P.M.

Calvin Coolidge
Coolidge Homestead is located in Plymouth. Administered by Vermont Division for Historic Preservation. Open daily 9:30 A.M. to 5:30 P.M. from mid-May to mid-October.

VIRGINIA

William Henry Harrison
Berkeley is located on Virginia Route 5, Charles City County, near Sherwood Forest. Owned privately, but the ground floor is open to visitors. Open daily from 8 A.M. to 5 P.M.

Thomas Jefferson
Monticello is located two miles southeast of Charlottesville, on Virginia Highway 53. Owned and administered by the Thomas Jefferson Memorial Foundation. Open daily March 1 to October 31 from 8 A.M. to 5 P.M. Open daily November 1 to February 28 from 9 A.M. to 4:30 P.M. Closed Christmas Day.

James Madison

Montpelier is located on State Highway 20, about four miles west of Orange. Privately owned, except for the Madison family cemetery, it is not open to the public.

James Monroe

Ashlawn is located two and a half miles from Monticello, near Virginia Routes 53 and 795, Charlottesville. Administered by the College of William and Mary. Open daily, from 9 A.M. to 6 P.M. March through October, 10 A.M. to 5 P.M. November through February. Closed Thanksgiving, Christmas and New Year's Day.

Oak Hill is located on U.S. Highway 15, about one mile north of U.S. 50 and about 8 miles south of Leesburg. Privately owned, it is not open to the public, except by special invitation to scholars.

John Tyler

Sherwood Forest is located on John Tyler Memorial Highway, Charles City County, 18 miles west of Williamsburg. It is owned by Mr. and Mrs. Harrison R. Tyler. Open daily, except Christmas Day, from 9 A.M. to 5 P.M.

George Washington

Mount Vernon is located on George Washington Memorial Parkway, seven miles south of Alexandria. Owned and administered by the Mount Vernon Ladies' Association. Open daily March 1 to October 31 from 9 A.M. to 5 P.M. Open daily November 1 to February 28 from 9 A.M. to 4:30 P.M. Closed on Christmas Day.

Washington Birthplace is located east of State Highway 3, about 38 miles east of Fredericksburg. Administered by the National Park Service. Open 9 A.M. to 5 P.M. seven days a week. Closed Christmas Day.

Woodrow Wilson

The Birthplace Manse is located at 24 North Coalter Street, Staunton. Administered by the Woodrow Wilson Birthplace Foundation, Inc. Open daily from 9 A.M. to 5 P.M. except Sundays of December, January and February: Thanksgiving, Christmas and New Year's Day.